SERVICE LEVEL MANAGER

BCS, THE CHARTERED INSTITUTE FOR IT

BCS, The Chartered Institute for IT champions the global IT profession and the interests of individuals engaged in that profession for the benefit of all. We promote wider social and economic progress through the advancement of information technology, science and practice. We bring together industry, academics, practitioners and government to share knowledge, promote new thinking, inform the design of new curricula, shape public policy and inform the public.

Our vision is to be a world-class organisation for IT. Our 70,000 strong membership includes practitioners, businesses, academics and students in the UK and internationally. We deliver a range of professional development tools for practitioners and employees. A leading IT qualification body, we offer a range of widely recognised qualifications.

Further Information
BCS, The Chartered Institute for IT,
First Floor, Block D,
North Star House, North Star Avenue,
Swindon, SN2 1FA, United Kingdom.
T +44 (0) 1793 417 424
F +44 (0) 1793 417 444
www.bcs.org/contact

http://shop.bcs.org/

SERVICE LEVEL MANAGER
Careers in IT service management

John Sansbury

Published by BCS Learning & Development Ltd, a wholly owned subsidiary of BCS, The Chartered Institute for IT, First Floor, Block D, North Star House, North Star Avenue, Swindon, SN2 1FA, UK. www.bcs.org

ISBN: 978-1-78017-294-1
PDF ISBN: 978-1-78017-295-8
ePUB ISBN: 978-1-78017-296-5
Kindle ISBN: 9-781-78017-297-2

Ebook available

British Cataloguing in Publication Data.
A CIP catalogue record for this book is available at the British Library.

Disclaimer:
The views expressed in this book are of the author and do not necessarily reflect the views of the Institute or BCS Learning & Development Ltd except where explicitly stated as such. Although every care has been taken by the author(s) and BCS Learning & Development Ltd in the preparation of the publication, no warranty is given by the author or BCS Learning & Development Ltd as publisher as to the accuracy or completeness of the information contained within it and neither the author nor BCS Learning & Development Ltd shall be responsible or liable for any loss or damage whatsoever arising by virtue of such information or any instructions or advice contained within this publication or by any of the aforementioned.

BCS books are available at special quantity discounts to use as premiums and sale promotions, or for use in corporate training programmes. Please visit our Contact Us page at www.bcs.org/contact

Typeset by Lapiz Digital Services, Chennai, India.

CONTENTS

LIST OF FIGURES AND TABLES

AUTHOR

From 1991 to 1997 John Sansbury worked with London Electricity plc (now EDF), during which time, as service level manager, he negotiated and drafted the service level agreements between IT and the five business units. This work included devising the performance management and reporting framework to underpin the process and drive improvements.

In 1997, with Compass Management Consulting (now part of the ISG-One Group) John became global head of practice for service management. In this role, he advised corporate clients globally on good service management practice in all its aspects, including service level and performance management.

In 2011, John founded Infrassistance Development Limited, an IT consultancy and training company and creator of 'ITIL®[1] In A Day', the world's only one-day, classroom-based ITIL Foundation course. He has since advised and worked with a multitude of clients in both the public and private sector on good practice with regard to service level management.

Between 2011 and 2013, John Sansbury and Colin Rudd, an ITIL author, co-developed the ITIL process self-assessment maturity model for the Cabinet Office/Axelos.

John is passionate about good service level management practice since he believes it forms the foundation of an effective and mutually beneficial relationship between IT and

---

[1] ITIL® is a registered trademark of Axelos Ltd.

its stakeholders. For decades, he has been promoting the idea that internal IT teams should become more professional in the delivery of services to their internal customers. This means adopting many of the practices employed by managed service providers.

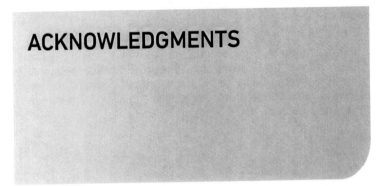

ACKNOWLEDGMENTS

Permission to reproduce extracts from ISO/IEC 20000-2:2012 from British Standards on pp. 69–72 has been granted by BSI Standards Limited (BSI). No other use of this material is permitted. British Standards can be obtained in PDF or hard copy formats from the BSI online shop: http://shop.bsigroup.com/

The SFIA codes and their associated definitions of core SLM skills on pp. 108–10 are reproduced with kind permission from SFIA (www.sfia-online.org).

ABBREVIATIONS

AST	agreed service time
BRM	business relationship manager
BYOD	bring your own device
CAB	change advisory board
CFO	chief finance officer
CIO	chief information officer
COBIT	Control Objectives for Information and Related Technologies
CSF	critical success factor
CSI	continual service improvement
DIKW	data, information, knowledge, wisdom
DT	downtime
HR	human resources
ITIL	(formerly an acronym of) Information Technology Infrastructure Library
KPI	key performance indicator
OLA	operational level agreement
PDA	personal digital assistant
PRINCE2	PRojects IN a Controlled Environment
SDM	service delivery manager

SFIA	Skills Framework for the Information Age
SIAM	service integration and management
SIP	service improvement plan or programme
SIPOC	supplier, input, process, output, customer
SLA	service level agreement
SLM	service level manager
SMART	Specific, Measurable, Achievable, Relevant, Timely
SMS	service management system
UC	underpinning contract

GLOSSARY

Critical success factor (CSF)   Something that must happen if an IT service, process, plan, project or other activity is to succeed.

IT service management   The implementation and management of quality IT services that meet the needs of the business.

ITIL framework   A long-established, mature and globally adopted library of practical guidance focusing primarily on the 26 key processes associated with IT service management. It was first published in 1989 and was preceded by Government Information Technology Infrastructure Management (GITIM). It was commissioned by the Office for Government Commerce (OGC) to identify and document good practice in the management and delivery of IT services.

Key performance indicator (KPI)   A metric that is used to help manage an IT service, process, plan, project or other activity. Key performance indicators are used to measure the achievement of critical success factors. Many metrics may be measured, but only the most important of these are defined as key performance indicators and used to actively manage and report on the process, IT service or activity. They should be selected to ensure that efficiency, effectiveness and cost effectiveness are all managed.

Operational level agreement An agreement between two teams or functions within the service provider that are intended to support the service level agreement.

Process owner The person who is held accountable for ensuring that a process is fit for purpose.

Service improvement plan (or programme) A document that identifies and helps the service provider to manage improvements relating to service provision and underpinning technology.

Service level Measured and reported achievement against one or more service level targets; alternative term for 'service level target'.

Service level agreement A negotiated agreement that documents the commitments made by both the service provider and their customer in association with the provision and consumption of services.

Service level requirement A requirement that a customer or sponsoring entity for a new or changed service may have for the service. Identifying service level requirements is typically the first step in establishing service level agreements as it identifies the requirements that the service provider will either agree in the service level agreement or negotiate in association with cost or price prior to reaching agreement.

Service management system The core of the ISO/IEC 20000 requirement that an organisation creates to define its approach to service management.

Service owner A role responsible for managing one or more services throughout their entire lifecycle.

Service provider An organisation supplying services to one or more internal or external customers.

Underpinning contract A document defining the formal agreement between the service provider and their supplier(s) for the provision of services that underpins the service provider's ability to meet its service level agreements with its customers.

INTRODUCTION

It is not at all uncommon for people to be appointed to a job or role with little more than a job description to guide them on the purpose and objectives of the role (and sometimes even that is absent). Regardless of whether the role of service level manager (SLM) is a new or existing one, as the role holder, you will need more than a job description to make a success of it.

Having held this position for a number of years, I am delighted to be given the chance by BCS to help you in this role. If you are such a person, or aspire to be one, my hope is that this book will provide you with useful information in support of both establishing a professional and valued service level management process and an enjoyable role that will contribute to a mutually beneficial relationship with your business colleagues and further your career.

I hope this book is equally relevant to your colleagues who depend on the success of your role, including your peers and managers. By taking a considered and professional approach to your role, you can absolutely make a positive and lasting contribution to the management and delivery of efficient and effective IT services.

An effective SLM is a vital asset for a customer-focused IT provider. The management and delivery of quality IT services is most often undertaken through application of the ITIL framework. This is a long-established, mature and globally adopted library of practical guidance focusing primarily on the 26 key processes associated with service management. The service level management process is one of these ITIL processes and it is instrumental in developing an effective relationship between service provider and customer. Get it right and just about everything that IT does thereafter can and should be focused on meeting the agreed and documented requirements of the business community, encapsulated in the service level agreements (SLAs).

Yet it can be challenging to find guidance for your role or for the organisation expecting positive and lasting results from it.

The role of an SLM spans both IT and its stakeholders and is instrumental in managing business requirements and expectations. If you carry it out effectively, it can enhance the perception of IT as a competent and professional service provider. It is one of a relatively small number of IT roles that shouldn't be founded on a purely technological capability but requires the classic business skills of communication, negotiation, patience and understanding, as well as the support you receive from your colleagues, peers and the senior IT leadership team.

Despite the fact that most organisations recognise the value of service level management as a process, they still find it challenging to adopt, particularly if the SLM lacks the skills, experience or authority within the organisation.

While the focus of this book is primarily on the role of the SLM within an internal service provider, the responsibilities and concepts are entirely relevant within a managed service environment, where the role tends to be referred to as service delivery manager (SDM). However, the two should be considered synonymous, and if you are in this role, please consider the principles to be equally relevant.

From an organisational perspective, setting up and managing both the service level management process and the SLM role are activities littered with trip wires. Common mistakes I've seen include the SLM opening discussions with stakeholders about their service level requirements and even starting to draft the SLA before being aware of IT's performance capabilities and limitations – an approach almost certainly doomed to failure.

I've also seen, on many occasions, documents masquerading as SLAs that are, in practice, what is often referred to as a 'declaration of intent' or 'definition of service'. The difference is that an SLA should be negotiated and should satisfy both the customer's and the service provider's objectives, whereas the declaration of intent or definition of service is a unilateral, one-sided commitment offered by one party to the other on an implied 'take it or leave it' basis.

Other tenets of good practice that I have seen broken are:

- making commitments that can't be measured;
- failing to report performance against agreed service levels;
- using inappropriate penalties to compensate for missed service levels;
- failing to review service levels on a regular basis such that they become shelfware and therefore increasingly less relevant;
- writing SLAs in IT-speak rather than using language meaningful to business users (for example, the classic statement around a service level committing to '99.9 per cent availability' when what a customer really wants to know is how many actual minutes of downtime a month this represents);
- failing to ensure that contracts with suppliers underpin and are aligned to the IT service provider's commitments in the SLAs.

As an effective SLM, you will recognise and manage these potential hazards, guide your organisation through them and build an increasingly closer and mutually beneficial relationship between yourselves as the service provider and your customers.

I write this book to share with you advice and guidance on the effective definition and performance of this role, based on a combination of my own personal experience, including my successes and mistakes and subsequent learning, as well as the wealth of documented good practice included within the ITIL framework. For a practising or aspiring SLM, the aim of this book is to help you to develop your role into an effective contributor to the delivery of a professional and valued service.

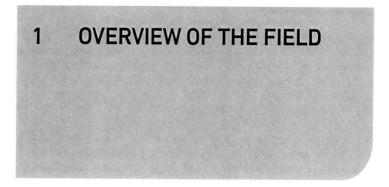

1 OVERVIEW OF THE FIELD

The purpose of this chapter is to position service level management within the wider context of service management. It is here that we introduce the concept of putting processes under control in order to ensure their repeatability, efficiency and effectiveness.

INTRODUCTION TO THE FIELD

The ability of an IT service provider to deliver consistent, reliable, efficient and effective services is dependent on a number of prerequisites. Few of these are more relevant and important than the maturity of its service management processes in general and the service level management process in particular. This is because this process ensures that the operational activities necessary to deliver efficient and effective services are recognised, understood, clearly defined and under control.

Process maturity is in effect a measure of the extent to which processes are under control. And if processes are not under control, then the services that they underpin are unlikely to be under control. This in turn impacts the ability of the service provider to meet the objectives of their stakeholders who depend on receiving effective services tailored to their needs. (Process maturity is covered in more depth in Chapter 10.)

If you doubt the value or question the investment necessary to have IT processes under control, ask an IT user about the extent to which they're happy with the services. If they say

'It depends', for instance on which service they use or when they use it or who they talk to in IT to get something done, then the processes are not under control. That means that the service to the user community is inconsistent, sub-optimised and therefore less than fully effective.

A lack of process or processes with inadequate control means activities are more reliant on individuals. Instead of the activities being undertaken according to defined procedures, there is variance, and variance is the enemy of effective service provision. If knowledge is retained in people's heads rather than in the service knowledge management system, then activities are conducted according to personal preferences or beliefs.

An analogy would be going to a restaurant and ordering your favourite dish but finding that what you were served was largely dependent on which chef was at work that day, or visiting a travel agent to book a holiday and having your destination, travel arrangements and the price of your holiday depend on the representative making the arrangements.

In my 45 years' experience of working with IT departments, it is sad but true that many departments still struggle to offer consistent, predictable and reliable services aligned to the needs of their business and stakeholders.

The key to be able to do so is shown in Figure 1.1. The generic activities associated with all processes are defined in the 'Process' box in the middle. The ability to ensure that these processes are undertaken on a consistent basis, aligned to stakeholder requirements, is achieved through essentially three control aspects:

- having a process owner accountable for the process (see 'The service level manager and the service level management process owner' in Chapter 2);

- having a written and agreed policy for the management of the process (see Appendix B);

- having clearly defined objectives for the process and a measurement framework to demonstrate the level of achievement and provide the basis of continual process improvement (see 'Measuring and reporting service performance' in Chapter 5).

Figure 1.1 Generic process control

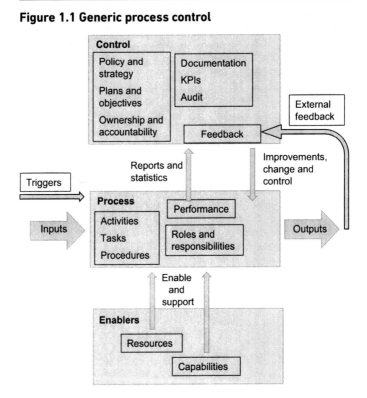

Service level management is often considered the most important process in the ITIL framework. This is because the main deliverable, the SLA, provides business users with a degree of confidence that their service provider understands and will provide the services and service performance necessary to support their business activities and processes.

For the service provider, arguably everything that the IT department does and those within it do should be aligned with or linked to the requirements defined in the SLA. In effect, it provides the menu for the delivery of services.

Having a clear definition of the services, service levels and responsibilities that the service provider and their customer commits to is one of the cornerstones of adopting a professional approach to service level management. In a managed service environment, this is driven by a contract, but the internal equivalent is the SLA that represents the start point and the lynchpin of good service management from which positive and mutually beneficial relationships can develop.

For each service management process, ITIL defines three roles:

- The process owner. This is the role accountable for the process in terms of establishing the process strategy and policy, its objectives and how it will be measured. These are the preliminary activities necessary to define how the process will operate. The process owner is also responsible for promoting the use of the process, providing the relevant training and awareness and, on an ongoing basis, auditing the process for efficiency and effectiveness and looking for ways to improve the process.

- The process manager(s). For service level management, this is the SLM role (or the SDM in a managed service environment) and the focus of this book. This role is responsible for managing and overseeing the day-to-day activities associated with the management of the process within the terms of reference established by the process owner.

- The process practitioner(s). The practitioners are the individuals or team carrying out the day-to-day activities under the direction of the process manager(s).

If the organisation has a single IT department (i.e. operating as a shared services environment), the roles of process owner and process manager are often assigned to a single individual. So, while this book is aimed at the SLM/SDM or process manager role, many process managers will also be assigned the process owner role. While there are clear demarcation lines, it is nonetheless important to recognise that for those of you who intend to use the guidance in this book to understand and improve the effectiveness of the SLM/SDM role, this is clearly influenced by the strategy, policy and objectives defined by the process owner.

If no process owner has been assigned (not at all an uncommon situation), the likelihood is that, by default, as the SLM/SDM you will be fulfilling at least part of the responsibilities of the process owner. For example, it would normally be the process owner who defines the structure of the SLAs, that is, customer-based or service-based. It would be the process owner who defines the key performance indicators (KPIs) for the process and how performance is reported. With no process owner in place, you will need to make these decisions.

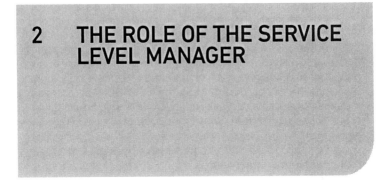

2 THE ROLE OF THE SERVICE LEVEL MANAGER

In this chapter, we look at the specific objectives, aspects, requirements and skills associated with the role and in particular, its differentiation from that of the related but distinct role of business relationship manager (BRM).

INTRODUCTION

The role of the SLM is arguably one of the most important roles in IT. This is because it is instrumental in promoting positive relationships between the service provider and the service provider's customers. It does this by providing a communications bridge between the two parties, aiming to ensure that IT services and the associated service levels remain aligned to the needs of business users and their departments.

Of course, as an IT service provider, your organisation may be providing services to internal customers, external customers or a combination of the two. Traditionally the SLM role is associated with the provision of services to internal customers. However, if customers are external, while the role is still appropriate, it takes on somewhat different characteristics since the relationship is on a commercial footing. In this case, the role of SLM may sit alongside or even be part of the role of account manager, since in a commercial relationship, service and finance are closely linked.

Nonetheless, even when the IT service provider's customers are internal and no money actually changes hands, there is no good reason why the management of service levels and indeed service provision should not be undertaken on a professional basis, and this is a recurring theme throughout this book.

From this point forward I will, for convenience, refer to the SLM role, but please consider the guidance to be equally applicable to the SDM role, unless otherwise stated.

PURPOSE OF THE ROLE

For the service level management process to be considered under basic control in the process maturity model, that is, at level 3 or 'defined' maturity (see Chapter 10), there should be a written policy relating to service level management. In the event that this exists, it will provide a useful blueprint for your role as SLM. Should it not exist, you may find it useful and appropriate to draft one yourself to gain both corporate commitment and legitimacy of the process (and implicitly your role). A draft policy template is offered in Appendix B.

A key purpose of your role as SLM is to understand, capture and respond appropriately to your customer's service level requirements on behalf of your organisation, which is acting as the IT supplier.

Your role is also instrumental in maintaining communication between IT and its customers in both directions, that is, providing information about IT services and capturing and acting on information about business requirements.

In fact, IT has two primary responsibilities: providing IT services to its customers and helping its customers make the most effective use of the IT services.

The second of these is often overlooked, yet is a key aspect of the SLM role, albeit in concert with the business relationship management role. In other words, it isn't sufficient just to provide IT services; it is an inherent part of the IT supplier's obligation to help its customers and users gain maximum advantage from those services. One could argue that this is more applicable to the provision of services to internal customers, but there's no reason why a managed service provider or outsourcer should not make the same commitment.

In practice, this means:

- comparing customers' requirements with the capability of the IT department to meet those requirements;

- managing the gaps;

- negotiating agreements that satisfy both parties;

- promoting IT's focus on consistently and efficiently meeting the requirements;

- supporting continual service improvement.

While you may not personally deal with or be responsible for all of these aspects, you are accountable for ensuring each is realised. So, for instance, to determine the capability of the IT department to meet your customer's service level requirements you might engage with colleagues working in the capacity and availability management area. For financial assessment, you will need to talk with your finance manager or chief finance officer (CFO).

To satisfy this purpose you will need to meet the objectives associated with your role included in Table 2.1 later in this chapter.

COMPETENCIES, SKILLS AND KNOWLEDGE

The SLM role requires a blend of relationship management and people skills with technical skills that is relatively unusual in IT but perhaps shared with the roles of BRM and continual service improvement manager.[2] If you lack the relationship management and people skills, you will find it

---

[2] See the BCS books in the same series, *Business Relationship Manager* by Ernest Brewster and *Continual Service Improvement Manager* by David Whapples, for more information.

hard to build meaningful relationships with your customers, a key aspect of the role. However, lacking basic technical skills will put you at a disadvantage in building relationships with your IT peers.

Ideally, you will have a portfolio of competencies, skills and knowledge spanning a number of areas, such as:

- interpersonal and relationship skills, as the role of SLM is primarily a people-based one;
- an understanding of (but not necessarily expertise in) IT technologies;
- a deeper understanding of the capabilities of IT generally;
- a certain level of general business acumen to be able to empathise and converse with your opposite numbers in the business units;
- an understanding of the business environment and business sector in which your organisation operates in order to recognise and help manage the specific challenges your customers face.

Interpersonal and relationship skills

Interpersonal and relationship skills are the softer skills and attributes you will need in order to be able to build an effective relationship with your colleagues on both the customer and supplier sides of the business. While these can be honed over time, they tend to be personality traits you already have to one extent or another that make you suitable for this type of role. These skills include diplomacy, influencing and negotiation, building trust, ability to empathise, dependency and reliability, and integrity and confidentiality. Employers therefore often look for people who already have these skills, even if they do not have a service management background, since the technical skills and an understanding of the organisation and its business can be taught.

As an SLM, the success of your role is going to depend to a large extent on these interpersonal and relationship skills.

Diplomacy, influencing and negotiation skills

There will be occasions when your customer's demands and requirements are either unrealistic or unreasonable. Diplomacy and influencing and negotiating skills will help you to deal with these situations and find solutions or compromises satisfactory to both parties. Sometimes you need a core belief that a solution is possible, even if it isn't obvious, and it is this confidence that can help you to arrive at a compromise. This is why you need to have a level of influence within the organisation, but particularly within IT, as technical people are often good at saying things like 'It can't be done.' Instead, work on the old adage that 'Where there's a will, there's a way.' But simply going over someone's head to gain authority for an action (for instance) is unlikely to be the basis of an effective working relationship with people on whom you are likely to rely in the future!

IT technology skills

There is a question over the level of technical or technology skills required by an SLM and, as is often the case, there is no right or wrong answer. From my own personal perspective, my lack of technical IT skills was never a hindrance in my role. This is because my customers and the business unit managers were themselves not focused on technology.

However, there are those who believe technical skills (of at least a moderate level) are an asset or even a prerequisite for the role. What is certain is that a balance of skills is appropriate and that ideally you can have a mainly non-technical conversation with a business customer yet also have a broadly technical conversation with an IT colleague.

The challenge is that it is rare to find individuals equally comfortable in front of customers and IT people and, on this basis, I do not see a lack of strong technology skills as necessarily an inhibiter to the SLM role. On the other hand, someone with strong technology skills but weak business acumen is unlikely to be suited to the role.

The level of technology skills you require will in fact be driven by the technology skills of your customers. They will expect you to have at least as much knowledge as they do, and some of them will have come from a technology background.

If you don't feel your technical skills are adequate, there are two alternatives. Either acquire these through training or, alternatively, take along a colleague more conversant with technology when you meet an informed customer. There is no shame in a lack of technology skills, particularly if your business acumen is particularly well developed.

Business acumen

Business acumen can be defined as an understanding of what makes a company successful. It includes the drivers of profitability and/or cash flow and a market-focused understanding of the business and its interrelationships with its customers, suppliers and regulators, and with legislation.

From your perspective as an SLM, refer to your understanding of what makes your organisation successful and how IT generates and supports corporate success. Your ability to understand this, reflect it in the SLAs and facilitate a successful IT and business relationship based on it, is arguably a critical success factor (CSF) for the role and should therefore be a primary focus.

The level of business acumen you require is considerably more than you are likely to gain from an induction course, although this can be a useful starting point. There are then likely to be some generic factors you need to know that relate to all businesses but, more importantly, there are aspects you need to know that are specific to your business and the sector in which it operates.

This in turn touches on the key ITIL concepts of 'Value on Investment' and 'Return on Investment' that represent ways of justifying a course of action or proposed investment of money, time or effort.

In practice, business acumen is not easily acquired, but may come either from insight gained from long service with the organisation or some form of relevant study, such as an economics degree or MBA.

Generic skills

As SLM, you will benefit from the following generic skills together with an understanding of the specific activities of the organisation:

- the capability to be self-directed with good time management – this role is rarely micro-managed by its manager;
- excellent verbal and written skills for obvious reasons;
- the confidence and maturity to discuss important concerns and requirements with senior business representatives.

THE SERVICE LEVEL MANAGER AND THE SERVICE LEVEL MANAGEMENT PROCESS OWNER

As we saw in the previous chapter, if you work in a larger and more mature organisation, you may have two roles associated with the service level management process: the SLM and the service level management process owner. In such an organisation, there will implicitly be more than one SLM since otherwise the norm is for a single person to adopt both roles.

The key responsibilities of the process owner include:

- defining the process policy and objectives (see Appendix B);

- defining the measurement framework for the process (see 'Measuring and reporting service performance' in Chapter 5);

- writing the procedures and work instructions to ensure that the process activities are undertaken consistently, efficiently and effectively across the organisation;

- promoting and championing the process on behalf of all stakeholders;

- ensuring the process policies and procedures are followed and the objectives are being met;

- identifying and delivering improvements to the process.

The responsibilities of the SLM will be covered in the next chapter.

As the SLM, you will develop a close working relationship with the process owner. This is of course a two-way relationship, as your approach is likely to be significantly influenced by theirs, and they will look to you and your fellow SLMs to support them in their objectives and help them to identify improvement potential.

If no process owner has been appointed, then you are likely to be expected, either implicitly or explicitly, to wear both 'hats' and fulfil some or all of the responsibilities of both roles. However, the SLM role will consume significantly more of your time than that of process owner, which tends to require no more than a few hours or less a month.

WHERE SHOULD THE SERVICE LEVEL MANAGER ROLE SIT WITHIN IT?

It is a fact of life that in some organisations, your authority as the SLM role holder is based on your position in the management hierarchy, and this is why it is important that your role is positioned such that it can drive the required actions within both the IT and the business departments.

This most likely precludes your role being at the level of junior management since, if you can't act as the voice of IT and drive the necessary actions to agree and deliver against your customer's service level requirements, your business colleagues will simply go over your head. While as the SLM you may not have the authority to negotiate service levels yourself, in taking your customer's service level requirements back into IT for evaluation you are acting as your customer's representative.

It may be, for instance, that your customer's new or changed requirements demand additional capacity, financial investment, extra resources or some other change. Your role is to act as the voice of your customer in requesting and promoting the change. In practice, this means you are providing an interface between your customer and their business activities and your colleagues within IT to help them understand the business drivers and benefits. In reverse, you also need to recognise the IT consequences of the change and may need to negotiate the associated costs and time frame with your customer. Both of these perspectives require an appropriate level of authority.

There are two risks associated with placing the role in the IT hierarchy. First, place it too low and the role has insufficient authority to drive the required actions. Second, in a highly technically focused IT organisation, the role of the SLM, which is essentially a people/service-focused role, can lack the respect and support of the other IT teams if it isn't placed at a sufficiently senior level within the management hierarchy.

The second risk is increasingly less likely as IT departments recognise the need to support the business and business processes, but it can still occur. Therefore, in smaller organisations, the SLM role may well report to the head of IT. In larger organisations, it is perhaps more appropriate to have the role one level lower in the hierarchy, reporting perhaps to the service manager or equivalent role.

SEPARATION FROM THE BUSINESS RELATIONSHIP MANAGER ROLE

The ITIL framework now recognises another relationship management role, that of BRM. The distinction between these roles can be blurred in some organisations and the same person may fulfil both in smaller organisations, so it's worth summarising the similarities and differences between the two roles (Table 2.1).

Table 2.1 Comparison of the business relationship management and service level management roles

Aspect	Service level manager	Business relationship manager
Purpose	Ensure that services both current and planned are delivered consistently and aligned to agreed service levels.	Establish and maintain an effective business relationship between the service provider and their stakeholders based on understanding stakeholder needs.
	Respond appropriately to missed service levels.	Ensure that the IT provider can meet stakeholder needs as these change over time.
	Proactively offer improved service levels where these are consistent with customers' willingness and ability to pay for them.	Help the business to make the most effective use of the IT services.
	Ensure that IT can meet agreed service levels both efficiently and effectively.	Ensure that services are provided at an appropriate price.

(Continued)

Table 2.1 (Continued)

Aspect	Service level manager	Business relationship manager
Objectives	Operational and tactical, for example: • recognise customers' requirements and the responsibilities of both parties in meeting these and, when agreed, document these in SLAs; • ensure that all services have specific and measurable service levels; • monitor and report performance against service levels, the reasons for any missed service levels and actions being taken to prevent recurrence; • provide a focal point for negotiating, renegotiating and updating SLAs; • support the continual improvement of services.	Tactical and strategic, for example: • understand stakeholders' perspectives of service and respond to changes in business strategy; • maintain customer satisfaction; • recognise and respond to changes in the customer environment; • identify and promote technology changes; • ensure that services remain relevant and aligned to business objectives and regulatory and legislative requirements; • act as a point of escalation in the event of complaints and/or disputes.
Engagement level	SLA signatories, for example department/ divisional heads.	Senior stakeholders, for example 'C' level executives and corporate heads.
Planning horizon	Typically, one to twelve months.	Typically, three months up to three or more years.

3 RESPONSIBILITIES, INTERFACES AND DEPENDENCIES

This chapter describes the responsibilities of the SLM role and the key relationships with other roles and processes. The first section associates the role with two of the five phases of the ITIL service life cycle, which is illustrated in Figure 3.1.

Figure 3.1 Five phases of the ITIL service life cycle

Service Strategy	• What services can we offer and to which customers? • How can we differentiate our services from our competitors? • Development of service management as a strategic asset • Promotion of sound governance and management of risk
Service Design	• Creation of new and changed services and solutions • Deliver expected performance, functionality and benefits
Service Transition	• Bridge the development/operations gap • Validation of design phase integrity • Consideration of operational requirements • Retirement of redundant services
Service Operation	• Provision of live services at agreed service levels • Delivery of value to stakeholders • Foundation for service improvements
Continual Service Improvement	• Alignment of services to changing business needs • Increase efficiency and effectiveness

RESPONSIBILITIES

To achieve the objectives of your role, you will likely have a number of responsibilities. Recognising that service level management is a service design process, these responsibilities blend proactive activities undertaken as part of the design of new and changed services and solutions with operational activities aimed at maintaining the alignment between customer and business requirements and IT service provision.

Service design-related responsibilities

The service design-related responsibilities of the role include the following.

- Discussions with customers and gathering and documenting their service level requirements for new services and service levels to ensure a clear understanding of the business requirements against which IT needs to deliver.

- Speaking with the business analyst to ensure a common understanding of the customer's requirements and supporting them in defining an accurate specification of requirements for the design team.

- Liaising with IT colleagues to understand the viability, cost and timescale to achieve the service level requirements for new services in order to manage customer expectations and reach a mutually agreeable and affordable solution. For instance, the SLM can engage with the application management team when a new or changed service is being designed to provide details of the required service levels that will need to be designed into the solution.

- Agreeing the structure and format of SLAs and drafting them.

- Understanding internal dependencies between teams and functions within IT, documenting these within operational level agreements (OLAs) and reviewing and updating them as necessary to ensure that the internal supply chain is capable of supporting the service level commitments with customers and IT users.[3]

---

[3] For the avoidance of doubt and confusion, it is worth recognising that in ITIL and in this book, 'users' or 'IT users' refer to people who consume IT services; and 'customers' typically refer to those people who pay for the service, that is, the person with the budget who signs off purchase orders and invoices. An individual fulfilling a customer role could, of course, consume IT services and therefore also be a user.

- Working with other IT teams, roles and processes to proactively prevent service issues, reduce risks and improve service quality to maximise the business value IT can provide.

- Sharing responsibility with the supplier manager to ensure that contracts with third parties are aligned with the SLAs with customers to support the achievement of customer-facing service levels.

Service operation-related responsibilities

The service operation-related responsibilities of your role include the following:

- meeting with your customers and gathering and documenting their service level requirements for changed services and service levels to ensure that these remain relevant and aligned to changing business requirements;

- liaising with the BRM(s) (where this role exists) in order to maintain a consistent business/IT interface that adds value to both parties;

- liaising with your IT colleagues to understand the viability, cost and timescale to achieve the service level requirements for changed services and service levels, as in service design, to manage customer expectations and reach a mutually agreeable and affordable solution;

- reviewing and updating SLAs on an annual or as-needed basis to ensure these remain relevant and drive positive behaviour by both parties to the agreement;

- producing or working with the service owner to produce service reports to validate performance against service levels and to understand and review the reasons for missed service levels;

- meeting with your customers and business representatives to review performance, explain any variations to them and capture any new or changed requirements to maintain positive relationships based on delivering appropriate levels of service;

- creating and managing service improvement plans for dealing with both reactive (for example, from missed service levels) and proactive (for example, where a potential improvement is identified) improvements to maximise the value that IT can provide and to help your customers and their business make the most effective use of IT services;

- working with your colleagues in other IT teams, roles and processes to proactively prevent service issues, reduce risks and improve service quality, again to maximise the value the business receives from IT;

- together with the supplier manager, reviewing third-party contracts for continued alignment with SLAs to identify and manage any discrepancies and inconsistencies; and

- providing a point of contact for your customers in order to improve their satisfaction with IT services and to deal with any complaints they may have about the service and/or its delivery.

These responsibilities form the template for Chapters 4 and 5, where the associated activities are given.

INTERFACES AND DEPENDENCIES

In the world of service management, there are interfaces and mutual dependencies between almost all processes. In this section, the most important interfaces relevant to service level management are identified, that is, those which are of most relevance to you in your role as SLM.

Business relationship management

In smaller IT departments of typically fewer than 100 people, there may not be separately defined SLM and BRM roles, as previously mentioned. In this case, as the role holder, you may be expected to wear two 'hats' and contribute to or perform both roles. For further information on how the purpose and objectives of these roles differ, please see Table 2.1.

These two roles vary in three ways:

- the level of business stakeholder with whom you will engage;
- the planning horizon;
- the focus on IT outcomes.

Against the first item, as SLM, you will be liaising with business representatives to understand and agree service levels. These people are typically department heads with the authority to sign an SLA. As BRM, your engagement with business representatives is higher up the food chain and likely to be with the most senior stakeholders. These may be enterprise representatives, for instance board or senior executive members.

In terms of the planning horizon, as SLM, you and your opposite numbers will typically be looking back at events that took place since the last service review and looking forward perhaps two to three months, with a typical maximum perspective of 12–18 months. The planning horizon of the BRM role is more likely to be one to five years and the focus is probably more on looking forwards than backwards.

As SLM, the focus of your customer is likely to range from the operational to the tactical. In other words, their interest will relate to operational performance and service delivery against service levels, extending to the processes and methods to ensure they receive reliable and consistent service delivery.

As BRM, the focus of your business colleagues is strategic. They will want to ensure that IT recognises its role in supporting the business strategy and how well placed IT is to maintain this support in the changing business environment.

Both roles share a responsibility for maintaining customer satisfaction and dealing with complaints.

Both roles must develop effective lines of communication with their IT colleagues since it is vital that, in either role, you are fully aware of current issues and challenges. There is nothing more embarrassing or guaranteed to undermine your role than when you're with a customer and they ask, 'So what's happening about the major incident?' and you have to reply, 'What major incident?'

Service catalogue management

Good practice requires the service catalogue to be produced before the SLAs. The catalogue represents the service provider's capabilities and shows how IT delivers value through services to its customers. Where SLAs are aligned to business units – that is, your organisation has customer-based SLAs – the SLA with each customer describes the services and service levels provided to that customer, which are usually a subset of the services identified in the service catalogue.

In practice, the SLAs usually precede the service catalogue since service level management tends to be a more mature process than service catalogue management and therefore an SLM is appointed before a service catalogue manager.

In this case, as the SLM, you may be asked to draft the service catalogue since, implicitly, its scope is the live services currently provided to the business which you have documented or will be documenting in the SLAs.

In a more mature environment, updates to the service catalogue are typically triggered by two activities: the introduction of a new service, initiated by service portfolio management;

or a change to an existing service, either requested by the customer or proposed by the service provider.

In the latter case, you should provide the necessary information to your colleague(s) managing the service catalogue to advise them of the service changes you have negotiated with the business.

In respect of both service catalogue management and service level management, it is worth recognising the three types of service that ITIL defines: core, enabling and enhancing services. Core services deliver the basic outcome required by customers. The enabling services are those that may or may not be visible to the customer but are necessary for the use of the core service. Enhancing services are not in any way essential to the delivery of the service but are added as excitement factors and can help to differentiate one service or service provider from another.

A good example of core, enabling and enhancing services is a train company whose core service is to take you to your destination safely and on time. The enabling services comprise the signalling, the stations and platforms, the power supply, the ticketing system and the timetable. The enhancing services might be the provision of Wi-Fi, food and on-board entertainment, none of which are necessary but add excitement and differentiate the service from a competitor's.

Capacity and availability management

A key activity in negotiating SLAs during the service design stage of the service life cycle is ensuring IT's ability to meet customers' requirements. In this respect, there are some processes and, by implication, some process managers with whom you are likely to develop a close working relationship. The objective is to clearly define the prerequisites necessary to meet the dimensions of the customer's new or changed requirements in terms of resources and capabilities. These will obviously include a financial dimension but also the technical configuration to support availability and performance requirements.

This may be an iterative procedure. Your customer may have specified their requirements and your colleagues in capacity and availability will use this information to determine the appropriate configuration. This in turn will determine the time and cost to achieve the requirements. With this information, your customer can make an informed decision whether to proceed or modify their expectations in the event that the cost and/or time and effort are unacceptable. The iteration continues until both parties agree. Of course the discussion might include suppliers, in which case the supplier manager is needed to engage the external organisations in the procedure and ensure the relevant commitments are enshrined in the contract with the supplier.

Once a service is operational, your interface with your colleagues in capacity and availability management is on a reactive basis, typically when a service becomes unavailable or performance deteriorates. While in the first instance it is likely to be the incident manager who will engage with colleagues in capacity and availability as part of the fault-finding and service restoration activities, you are clearly a stakeholder in this procedure and will want to be kept informed or have a discussion directly with the availability/capacity manager(s).

Incident management

Your relationship with the incident manager is likely to be the closest relationship you have beyond that with your customer(s). This is simply because once services are live and operational, the effectiveness of incident management and therefore implicitly the effectiveness of the incident manager role underpins the ability of IT to meet many of the key service levels defined in the SLAs, such as availability.

The cross-functional nature of the incident manager's role also allows them to keep you informed about the progress of incidents and what IT is doing to fix the incident so that you can keep your customers informed (this responsibility might be shared with the incident manager).

A proactive aspect of your relationship with your incident manager (and also the availability manager, who is accountable for planning and maintaining the availability of new and changed services, applications and components) is for them to advise on IT's ability to meet new or changed availability requirements requested by your customers. In order for you to understand what level of service is achievable in managing incidents, the incident manager will need to understand how to determine incident impact and urgency for your customer's new or changed service. This will ultimately help them appropriately prioritise such incidents based on the agreed responsiveness and fix times.

On a day-to-day basis, you are likely to spend more time with the incident manager(s) than with any other role, since together you share a key responsibility in terms of agreeing and meeting service levels (at least for availability). Furthermore, the incident manager can provide you with information about the progress in managing incidents, and you can provide them with information about the impact of the incident to help them prioritise or re-prioritise it appropriately.

Unfortunately, it is a surprisingly rare occurrence to find an organisation with an incident manager! In this case, you are likely to have to obtain the information from a combination of the service desk manager and perhaps the managers of each second-line resolver group.

Supplier management

Your relationship with the supplier manager or supplier management team is one of the closest between two process roles in the whole of IT. This is a natural consequence of the fact that the supplier manager has accountability for a key part of the supply chain. The commitment that IT makes in terms of providing services to its customers as described in the SLAs is almost always dependent to one extent or another on parallel or underpinning commitments with suppliers (sometimes referred to by ITIL as 'partners').

Put simply, if any part of the service offered by IT has any form of dependency on a supplier, then it is vital to understand the nature of that dependency and enshrine it in a contract with the supplier. Although the establishment and management of suppliers and contracts sits firmly with the supplier manager, as SLM you share with the supplier manager the responsibility for ensuring the alignment between supplier contracts and customer SLAs.

A simple example can illustrate this interface. If you make a commitment to a customer or department to provide a fully configured laptop within, say, 10 days of receiving an authorised request, you are likely to need the laptop supplier to deliver the actual laptop for IT to configure within perhaps five days. IT might then have three days to complete the configuration by installing corporate applications, antivirus software and standard personalisation elements, leaving two days to send the laptop to the user. Without the clearly defined and contractually enshrined supplier commitment, IT's commitment to its customer is meaningless.

The challenge you may find in this respect is that supplier management might be undertaken by a function outside IT, such as purchasing. You will therefore need to gain their buy-in to managing this alignment and indeed do so during the service design stage. An effective way of recognising this relationship is of course to establish an OLA with purchasing.

You will need to discuss the customer requirements with the supplier manager early enough in the set-up of a new or changed service that the contract can be signed before the service is offered to customers.

Often the supplier contracts are already in place, so one of your first activities upon taking up the SLM role is to validate to what extent the contractual commitments underpin IT's SLAs. If you identify a misalignment or missing aspects, you will need to bring this to the attention of the supplier manager as this is something for them to manage, albeit with your support in understanding the specific requirements.

As your relationship with the supplier manager develops over time, you might usefully be invited to proactively participate in the early stages of supplier selection and (for instance) the tendering process to proactively ensure that new contracts or contract updates include the appropriate references and commitments. This is one effective sign of a maturing service level management process.

Financial management

It is difficult to think of a situation where a service level is being negotiated or changed that does not have a financial perspective to it. You will therefore need to liaise closely with the finance manager so that they can advise and sign off any expenditure associated with your service level negotiations.

Design coordination

If this process is active in your organisation and someone has the responsibility for it, you will liaise with them during the design stage, that is, as you are negotiating new or changed service levels. Their objective is to ensure that all aspects of design in terms of the activities, processes and resources are coordinated in order to promote design efficiency and ensure that design activities conform to the organisation's design standards. If this process does not exist, then as the SLM, you will need to engage directly with relevant design processes and roles, such as availability and capacity management, yourself.

Continual service improvement

Continual service improvement (CSI) is a cross-functional activity that engages with all functional and process roles to operate as a centre of excellence and provide guidance to identify and manage efficiency and effectiveness improvements.

The role holder may be known as CSI manager or quality manager. Their primary perspective is the alignment of IT services with business requirements and objectives, and of course this overlaps with your perspective, making them a vital ally of yours.

Service owners

Service owners have the ultimate accountability for the service(s) they own. This includes:

- accountability for delivery of the service and ensuring associated service levels are met;
- acting as the primary customer contact for service enquiries;
- defining and conforming to service levels;
- effective monitoring, measurement and performance reporting of the service (although reporting to the customer is usually conducted by the SLM);
- the focus on service improvement;
- the accuracy of service information in the service catalogue;
- the escalation point for major incidents;
- participating in service review meetings; and
- representing the service in change advisory board (CAB) meetings.

You will see the potential for significant overlap with your role and it's therefore important to ensure a clear division of responsibilities, or at least an understanding of the overlap, so that the customer and users of the service are clear about who covers which aspects and therefore with whom to engage in each specific circumstance.

4 KEY ACTIVITIES ASSOCIATED WITH THE SERVICE DESIGN STAGE OF THE SERVICE LIFE CYCLE

Many of the most important activities undertaken by the SLM occur in the service design and service operation phases of the service life cycle. This chapter and the next therefore look at these activities in more detail.

The information in this chapter describes the main activities of the SLM during the service design phase of the service life cycle.

COORDINATING THE SERVICE DESIGN ACTIVITIES

If there is a design coordinator (or design coordination process manager) in your organisation, that person will take the primary role of coordinating the processes, resources and activities associated with the new or changed requirements. They will therefore act as the primary interface with the design and project teams and the other service design process managers on your behalf. If there is no design coordinator or design coordination process, then it might be appropriate for you to take on this role, since you effectively own the relationship with your customer.

ESTABLISHING OR VALIDATING THE MEASUREMENT AND REPORTING CAPABILITY

The extent to which this first step is necessary depends on the maturity of your organisation's existing capabilities. In my experience, many organisations are desperately immature in terms of having a meaningful and accurate service measurement framework in place. An effective way to start this activity or validate the extent to which it is fit for purpose is to build out the required measures from the vision, mission and objectives.

The start point is to recognise and document the organisation's or business's vision, mission and objectives. In order to achieve these, certain CSFs need to be met. Once these have been recognised from a business perspective, the IT equivalents need to be recognised.

The relationships are built downwards. In other words, the vision determines the CSFs, of which there should be a relatively small number, perhaps five to ten. In turn, the extent to which the CSFs are being achieved needs to be measured through the use of KPIs. For each CSF, there should be a small number of KPIs: two to five work well.

KPIs are typically one measure divided by another. For instance, productivity is number produced divided by number of production units. Error rate is total number produced divided by number of errors. Therefore, for each KPI there will be one or more measures (Figure 4.1).

Figure 4.1 Mapping the IT vision to the organisation's vision and developing the appropriate measurement framework

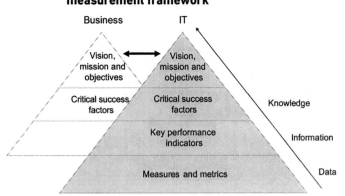

While these relationships are derived from a top-down perspective, their value lies in understanding how sometimes low-level measurements ultimately contribute to the realisation of the corporate mission. This approach is consistent with the ITIL DIKW (data, information, knowledge, wisdom) hierarchy and helps IT to understand what should be measured and its relevance in service delivery. Without this approach, the risk is that IT measures, and continues to measure, the things it *can* measure, rather than the things it *should* measure.

Clearly, the understanding of which measures to use at an IT level is likely to be beyond the scope of your role as SLM; however, you are a key stakeholder in the recognition, gathering and reporting of measures and KPIs. Indeed, the requirements of your customers that will ultimately be contained within the SLAs should be the basis of the measurement and reporting framework.

The key message here is to ensure that this recognition and capability exists *before* you commence the SLA negotiations. What you're trying to avoid by so doing is committing to levels of performance that can't even be measured.

The likelihood is that these activities may develop in parallel. In other words, as you start to gather requirements, IT needs to develop the corresponding measurement and reporting capabilities.

Another consideration around measurement and reporting is using meaningful measures, that is, those that customers and users recognise and ideally can use to control consumption. This is dealt with under 'Using meaningful measurements' in Chapter 5.

With regard to reporting, you need to understand the data sources, for example the service desk for information on incidents and change management for information on changes. It should not be your job to extract this data; rather you should receive it from the relevant teams as well as the service owners and compile them into a meaningful performance report. The data should be supplemented with explanations for any variance and corresponding preventative actions.

IDENTIFYING YOUR CUSTOMER

It may sound strange, but the prerequisite to establishing a successful relationship with your business colleagues via SLAs and service level management is to identify your customers, that is, the business people or user representatives who can define the service level requirements on behalf of the community they represent.

There is no formal guidance to be found on this in the service management frameworks and textbooks. A customer is anyone who represents a user community for whom IT provides a service. For practical purposes, your customers are likely to be grouped into teams or departments. It is for each organisation to identify the most appropriate people to fulfil this role.

When negotiating service-based SLAs, your customer is the person who can represent a customer group. If you are structuring your SLAs on a service-based model, then your customers are the people who can represent the service across multiple business units.

No matter what the size of your organisation, it is likely that there are a number of discrete business activities. If your organisation operates in the private sector, you are likely to have a finance department, a human resources (HR) team, a sales and marketing team and one or more operational teams conducting the prime activities. The fact that the operational teams might be field-based or office-based could also influence the selection of the person who will negotiate and sign the SLA on behalf of their function.

In both the private and public sectors, parts of your organisation might be aligned to specific stakeholder groups.

For instance, in the public sector, this might be different types of hospital patients or consumers of different council services. In the private sector, it might be groupings of policyholders in insurance. Alternatively, the organisational structure might reflect the separation of operational activities such as upstream and downstream in the petrochemical industry or investment and administration in banking.

Ideally, your customer groupings should reflect the organisational structure in a way that is natural and meaningful to your business colleagues.

Once you have decided on your customer grouping, you need to identify the individual who best represents that group. This is critical because that individual will be the person with whom you negotiate the SLA and who will sign the SLA on behalf of their user community. It therefore needs to be someone with the appropriate authority. It should also be the person you will meet at the regular service review meetings.

GATHERING AND DOCUMENTING CUSTOMERS' SERVICE LEVEL REQUIREMENTS

The purpose of this activity is to ensure a clear understanding of the business requirements against which IT and its suppliers need to deliver.

Customers' new or changed service level requirements represent the start point or one of the triggers for the service level management process. However, where these represent entirely new requirements or significant changes to existing arrangements, this should be treated as a service design activity, meaning that all the normal design considerations will apply, such as consideration of the investment decision, the production of a service design package and engagement with a business analyst.

In my experience, and at the risk of stating the obvious, there is no better way to gather and understand your customer's requirements than to ask them. Wherever practical, this is best done in a face-to-face meeting, not only because it's more effective than using a telephone or web-based facility but because it shows a level of commitment to them and the business on your part and therefore on IT's part. In meeting face to face you might also have an opportunity to see first-hand the customer operation and better understand the business objectives and pressures, which establishes the context for the service requirements.

How you document your customer's requirements is up to you. Some people prefer to take notes, others will use a voice recorder or even a voice recognition facility. If you use a voice recorder or a voice recognition facility, do ask your customer if they're OK with doing so first.

It is good practice to write up your notes into a formal service level requirements document, ask your customer to review this for accuracy and then sign it off, since the requirements are likely to form the basis of the SLA. This might be an iterative activity, particularly if this is the first time such discussions have happened. The requirements should also be filed and retained in the service knowledge management system using your organisation's document management system to ensure they are securely stored and version-controlled.

At this stage, you should not commit to basing the SLA on the customer's requirements because even in an internal relationship the technical considerations and the cost of meeting the requirements needs to be identified, maybe some options or alternatives considered and then put to the customer for sign-off or a second iteration.

DECIDING ON THE SERVICE LEVEL AGREEMENT STRUCTURE

Your first decision should be which SLA structure you will adopt. This can either be service-based, that is, where there is one SLA per service, negotiated with the customer representative(s) for that service; or customer-based, that is, where there is one SLA per customer for all the services they use. These structures are described below.

Figure 4.2 provides a simple illustration of the two primary SLA structures.

Figure 4.2 The main options for structuring SLAs

	Service-based SLA		
Service Customer	Email	Customer billing	Business application
Finance	✓	✓	✗
Marketing	✓	✗	✓
Human resources	✓	✗	✗

(Customer-based SLA: Finance, Marketing, Human resources rows)

There are other options. For instance, you might have a separate SLA with each customer for each service they use. This will result in a multitude of relatively short SLAs of only a few pages in length. The positive aspect is that it allows you to offer each customer a service level appropriate for their needs, and that it differs from customer to customer even for the same service. The downside is that you will have a multiplicity of documents to manage, sign and version-control.

The other extreme is to have a single SLA for all services and all customers. In practice, this option is only viable for small organisations with a few discrete services and a few customers, otherwise the SLA will run to potentially hundreds of pages and forever require reviewing and updating.

Service-based SLAs

In this option, there is one SLA per service. While this option is perfectly viable, there are two limitations you should recognise. First, in this structure, the service levels associated with the service usually need to be the same for each customer. If this is what you wish, this is not a drawback, but some organisations prefer to have the flexibility of offering different levels of service for different customers. Second, each SLA will have multiple signatories. In my experience, gaining a single customer's signature on the SLA can be challenging enough; having multiple signatories typically complicates and lengthens the process.

Customer-based SLAs

In this option, there is one SLA per customer that describes and references all of the services that the customer agrees to take. In contrast to the service-based SLA, this structure allows different levels of service for the same service to be offered to different customers. It also only requires one customer signature on each SLA. For these reasons, the customer-based SLA is the more common structure.

Multi-level SLAs

ITIL references multi-level SLAs, that is, SLAs that can contain a blend of either service- or customer-based SLAs with a corporate level commitment. Services subject to a corporate level SLA might include security, continuity or network provision, for instance, being services that are typically provided on a universal basis to all customers and at the same level of service. Such an agreement can be appended to a customer- or service-based SLA.

MANAGING AND INFLUENCING CUSTOMER REQUIREMENTS

One of the challenges you will face is being able to make things happen for your customers. Clearly it's not just a question of you being able to give them what they ask for, since that is unlikely to be within your remit. Rather, your role is to understand their requirements and act as their channel for submitting, assessing and sponsoring their requests.

In this respect, we're not talking about minor requests such as replacement PCs or additional licences. Rather this might be a new service, a revised service level or a major change in the way that a service is used. Perhaps there will be a new user department coming on-stream or they are considering a new version of their key business application.

Depending on the roles within your organisation, there is the potential for these types of requests to overlap with several roles. Major requests such as those above might in some organisations be placed via the account manager or BRM. Less significant requests might be handled as part of change management or request fulfilment. Other types of change might go through a project team. You will need to be clear about the protocol and procedures within your organisation so that you can advise your customers accordingly.

Assuming that you have the authority to receive and manage such requests on behalf of your customer, your objective is to fully understand the nature of the requirement and to feed back to your customer the feasibility, timescale and cost of meeting the requirement. In this respect, you will need to capture the requirements and pass these for consideration to the relevant departmental or functional managers. The requirements may have any number of technical as well as resourcing and finance implications. The likelihood is that your organisation already has a defined approach for managing such requests, depending on the scale. Your role is to effectively sponsor your customer's requirement within IT.

DEFINING SERVICE LEVELS

Defining and agreeing the appropriate service levels is a vital aspect of your role and therefore has its own chapter (Chapter 8). Its mention here indicates that it is the next step in the establishment of SLAs.

MEETING NEW OR CHANGED SERVICE LEVEL REQUIREMENTS

Unless your role is near the top of the IT department, you are unlikely to have the authority to sign off customers' service level requirements. Instead, the requirements need to be evaluated by a combination of internal IT teams.

Ideally, your organisation will have defined procedures and committees or investment boards for handling such requirements to ensure that they are aligned to the service portfolio and economically viable, and to determine the resources required and the delivery time frame. There may be more than one option for meeting the requirements and each should be evaluated and documented, since the final decision rests with your customer.

The actual IT teams involved might include the IT executive or steering group to validate that the required service is something the IT department wishes to offer. A good example of this would be support for customers using their own non-standard IT equipment such as tablets and wearable technology (bring your own device; BYOD).

Other IT teams that will need to be consulted are likely to include capacity and availability management in order to plan and cost the resources necessary to meet the customer's service levels. There may also be a need to consult those responsible for continuity management. Finally, IT finance will need to agree the funding to meet the required service levels and some form of cost recovery or charging method.

As we have already mentioned, the process of negotiating service levels is often an iterative one in that, if the projected cost of meeting the customer's service level requirements is prohibitive, the customer may moderate their requirements until an appropriate balance is struck.

A final checkpoint is that where a requirement is new, you must ensure that the capability of measuring performance and workload volumes exists or can be built into the solution so that you can measure and report against the corresponding service levels.

DRAFTING THE SERVICE LEVEL AGREEMENT

Once your customer has agreed and signed off the approach for meeting their requirements, you can start drafting the SLA. Since the SLA is a customer-facing document, you should draft it in a clear and unambiguous way and in 'plain English'.

There is no right or wrong way to draft an SLA; what's more important is that it contains the information necessary to describe the service or services within scope and the service levels associated with them.

The first section should contain the basic terms and conditions, that is:

- the names of the parties to the agreement;
- the start date for the agreement and the scheduled review date;
- the purpose of the agreement;
- the signatories and their positions within the organisation; and
- the version number and how changes to the agreement are controlled.

The main body of the SLA could usefully describe one service per page or section (on the assumption that the SLA is a customer-based structure) and define the following:

- the name and description of the service, that is, the value it provides and/or business processes and activities it supports;
- any prerequisites necessary for use of the service such as other applications or specific versions of hardware or licensing requirements;

- the scheduled availability of the service or service hours and whether or not the service is available at weekends and public holidays;

- details of any agreed maintenance periods when the service will either be unavailable or have restricted availability; and

- the means whereby the customer can request a change to any of the service levels.

A sample SLA is included as Appendix A.

ESTABLISHING OPERATIONAL LEVEL AGREEMENTS

The process for evaluating your customer's requirements will help to define the interdependency between internal teams. There will be some obvious generic dependencies, such as with the incident management, change management and request fulfilment teams as well as some service-specific dependencies related perhaps to specific databases, networks and web services. You are accountable for identifying these interdependencies, although it's worth recognising that the design coordination manager (if there is such a role in your organisation) can support you in this respect. You then have to decide whether or not these interdependencies justify creating an appropriate OLA for their management.

The concept of the OLA is similar to that of the 'SIPOC' (see below) in process improvement methods such as Six Sigma. It recognises that, typically, errors and mistakes occur when there is a hand-off between two teams or individuals and that an effective way to reduce such errors is to formally recognise the relationship between the teams.

SIPOC in Six Sigma refers to there being a Supplier that provides Input which is subsequently Processed by the recipient before they in turn pass the Output from their activities to their Customer. This approach introduces the concept of the internal supply chain. For example, the service desk might receive a request from a user for some new software. The service desk will validate the authenticity of the request and then pass it to the software asset management team for fulfilment. In turn the software asset management team may need to engage with the purchasing department to acquire the software. In order for the IT department to commit to a service level for fulfilling the request from the user, they may decide to document the responsibilities of each internal team in an OLA.

The OLA would describe what each team is expected to provide to the next, by when, and any special instructions necessary for subsequent steps. In this way, the obligations and commitments of each team are clearly defined and then documented within specific procedures in order to provide assurance of the performance of the activities and confidence that they will be carried out consistently, efficiently and effectively.

Ideally, the construction of the OLAs will be a role that is shared between the respective teams or departments with your advice and guidance. This helps to ensure the teams themselves recognise and adopt their responsibilities. Your advice and guidance will facilitate the OLA construct, ensure that it conforms to good practice and uses your organisation's standard document format and structure.

MANAGING SERVICE QUALITY, MAXIMISING BUSINESS VALUE

The IT department, as a supplier of IT services to its customers, has two responsibilities: to provide IT services in line with agreed customer requirements; and to help its customers and users make the most effective use of IT services.

The latter responsibility is often unrecognised but is a key characteristic of a mature IT department. This also references another such characteristic, namely a greater focus on proactive management. Taking these two attributes together requires IT to provide proactive advice and guidance to its customers and users about innovative ways to use the IT services for greater business benefit. This might be in the form of providing a competitive edge, delivering IT services in a new way, such as with the use of new technology, or simply using the IT and service resources more efficiently.

As SLM and by virtue of your close relationship with the business and business users, you have a key role in this respect, typically shared with the CSI (or quality) manager, the BRM(s) and the service owner(s).

From the customer/user perspective, it doesn't particularly matter where the advice comes from, as long as it is available and effective. You therefore need to work with your colleagues to this end and take particular responsibility for improvements that can offer improved service levels.

Another stakeholder in proactive improvement is the problem manager. The proactive aspect of their role is to identify and prevent incidents and problems from occurring and thereby improve IT's ability to meet the agreed service levels and indeed offer improved service levels. While the problem manager has the accountability for incident and problem prevention, your role is vital in helping them to understand the business perspective in terms of context, relevance and priority.

Many of your IT colleagues will have a technology focus, concentrating on the management and performance of storage media, transaction processing, application management or network management. They clearly have expertise and specific skills in their roles, but they may not always appreciate the business perspective. By working with them, you can help the IT department to channel their technology capabilities into delivering value through services and thus positive and lasting business benefits.

ALIGNING SERVICE LEVEL AGREEMENTS AND SUPPLIER CONTRACTS

An important part of the service design activity is to identify external suppliers and establish contracts with them for the supply of services and products. The ITIL framework does not yet define a single role for the end-to-end management of the supply chain, although the recognition of the importance of such governance in the management of multiple suppliers is now recognised within the service integration and management (SIAM) framework.

Therefore, although the accountability for suppliers rests with supplier management and the supplier or purchasing manager, you and they share the responsibility for ensuring the alignment of supplier contracts and SLAs. In this respect, as SLM, you must ensure that when new suppliers are on-boarded, the service levels within the corresponding contracts align with your customer's service level requirements.

A classic example is the provision of PCs. Many organisations offer a turnaround commitment for the provision of a new desktop or laptop PC in terms of a number of days between receiving an authorised request and supplying a pre-configured, fully functional and working device at the user's location.

Most organisations are reliant to one extent or another on third parties or suppliers to provide and deliver to IT the frame of the PC, after which IT will carry out the necessary work to complete the build to corporate standards by, for instance, pre-loading corporate application software, network connectivity, antivirus software and data encryption. In this context, the ability of the IT department to supply the pre-configured PC is critically dependent on the supplier to deliver the frame to IT.

Very often, the management of suppliers is undertaken not by the IT department but by the purchasing department, and contracts are awarded primarily on price considerations. As a consequence, there is no guarantee that the supplier contract has been tailored to meet the customer SLAs.

MEASURING SERVICE LEVEL PERFORMANCE

It is perhaps obvious, but worth saying nonetheless, that any commitment made by one party to another in an SLA must be measurable and must be reported, otherwise it is meaningless. Therefore, while you are drafting the SLA, you need to liaise with your colleagues in application management to ensure that the relevant measurement capability is either available or designed into the solution. Establishing the relevant KPIs and the metrics and measurements on which they are based is a service design activity, as witnessed by the fact that in the ITIL framework, measurement is one of the five key aspects of service design. If the measurement capability is not designed into the solution at this stage, it is typically much harder to retrofit it.

5 KEY ACTIVITIES ASSOCIATED WITH THE SERVICE OPERATION STAGE OF THE LIFE CYCLE

The information in this chapter describes the main activities of the SLM during the service operation phase of the service life cycle.

REPORTING PERFORMANCE

As already mentioned, it is obligatory that any commitments contained in an SLA must implicitly be measured and reported back to the customer. The ability to measure performance is a responsibility within the service design stage of the life cycle, but the reporting itself is a function of the service operation stage.

There are two leading practices to note in terms of reporting, the first of which we have already referenced: it is not part of your role as SLM to measure the performance achieved; rather it is the responsibility of the teams undertaking the actual activities. Your role is to collate these performance statistics, publish them and discuss them in the customer review meetings. The second practice is that reports should ideally comprise three key components: charts, values and narrative. Charts are designed to show trends and can also clearly indicate when a service level is missed. Values are necessary to satisfy those who are wary of charts and prefer definitive numbers. The narrative is the most important aspect of any report. The basic premise is that a report should be capable of being read without explanation. Therefore, the narrative should comment on and provide the underlying reasons for any exceptions or trends and any missed service levels.

With regard to the first practice, while it may be tempting to be in control of the end-to-end process of performance reporting, if you attempt to gather the actual performance statistics from the various operational teams responsible for delivering the service, this will consume a huge part of your time doing something for which you should not be responsible. It will also appear to absolve the operational teams from an important part of their responsibilities, since each team should be responsible for managing, reporting and improving the quality of their own work.

To provide the narrative, you may need to discuss the performance statistics with the operational team(s) that produced them in order to be able to brief your customer at the service review meetings on the reason(s) for a service level being missed and the actions being taken to prevent a further breach. Trends may be indicative of longer-term changes that you and your customers will also want to understand.

A simple guide is to consider the perspective of your customer: what would they want to know in terms of the service quality and consistency? In essence, your customers want confidence that their service provider is in control of the service, that the service is being delivered in a way consistent with its use, taking into account future requirements and that you are actively looking at improvements on an ongoing basis.

We look in more detail at service reporting in 'Measuring and reporting service performance' below.

MANAGING CHANGES TO SERVICES AND SERVICE LEVELS

Experience suggests that no sooner have you agreed the service levels and signed off the SLA than the customer's requirements change. 'Change is the only constant,' wrote Heraclitus of Ephesus (535–475 BC); so you will need to routinely and regularly validate your customer's requirements and be prepared to manage requests for changes to services and service levels.

The service review meetings you have with your customers are typically a source of new and changed requirements, but changes can and should also be driven proactively from within IT, often through CSI. They can also come from external sources such as legislative and regulatory changes.

It may be that the change is mandatory, but even then there's usually more than one way to implement it. The point is that, similarly to establishing the service levels in the first place, the procedure may be iterative before the agreed solution is deployed. At this point, though, the management of the change is likely to fall under the control of the change management process to ensure that all potential interfaces and dependencies are appropriately considered.

Once agreed and introduced, any such changes should be reflected within the service catalogue. As SLM your role is to advise the service catalogue manager of such changes. The changes also need to be reflected in the performance management system(s) and service level reporting, which is your responsibility.

LIAISING WITH THE BUSINESS RELATIONSHIP MANAGER(S)

When services are live and if your organisation has both the SLM role and the BRM role, then it is clearly important to ensure timely and effective communication between the two, and to avoid duplication. The main separation of the two roles is by stakeholder level, which is to say that the people with whom each role engages are usually different. Communication is vital to ensure that both roles have access to the same information flowing both in and out of IT and share their respective customer insights. One common way to manage this is through a customer relationship management system whereby either role can update the system for the benefit and information of the other.

REVIEWING AND MANAGING EXISTING SERVICE LEVEL AGREEMENTS

During your regular customer reviews (see 'Managing customer reviews' below), it is useful to have an agenda item that requires both parties to validate the continued relevance, accuracy and applicability of the SLA. Regardless, good practice requires you to formally review and validate the content of the SLAs at least once a year if a review has not been triggered in the meantime. If you do not do this, there is a danger that the SLAs become shelfware and fall into disuse as they become increasingly irrelevant. More importantly, there is an increasing likelihood that the services IT provides and the business requirements gradually go out of alignment and IT loses the trust of its customers. Therefore, an annual review should be a key requirement in the SLA itself.

If a review triggers a change to the SLA, this should again be formally managed through change management since the SLA is a version-controlled document and configuration item.

MANAGING SERVICE IMPROVEMENT PLANS/ PROGRAMMES

We have already mentioned that one of the often forgotten responsibilities of IT is to help its customers make the most effective use of their services. IT should therefore always be on the lookout for potential improvements, and the mechanism for managing these is referred to as the service improvement plan or programme (SIP).[4]

---

[4] The term 'service improvement plan' tends to be used to manage a one-off change for a specific purpose, whereas the term 'service improvement programme' tends to be used for an ongoing programme of improvements into which specific items are introduced as and when required. Confusingly, both are abbreviated to 'SIP'.

There will be occasions when, as SLM, you instigate a SIP in response to a customer need to change one or more current service levels. This may be reactive, in response to a missed service level, or proactive, for instance to improve competitiveness; but it may also be triggered by IT when the department identifies an opportunity for improvement. Occasionally, customers may propose a reduction in service levels if there is a price advantage. In any of these cases, the SIP is an effective way to manage such changes.

As an SLM, you are likely to own the SIP, in which case it will be your responsibility to recognise the need for one, gather the requirements, build the business case for change, coordinate the resources necessary, track the benefits and ensure that a post-implementation review is conducted.

Service improvement in a managed service environment

A common characteristic of a managed service environment is that the service provided is the minimum necessary to meet the agreed service levels. Yet those engaging the managed service provider frequently talk about a 'partnership' with their service provider.

There is no agreed definition of a partnership, but clearly it should involve more than the basic provision of a service consistent with agreed service levels. There are, though, aspects of a managed service that can move it towards a partnership, including the following.

- Operating an open-book accounting approach whereby the customer and service provider agree a level of profit that can be built into the service, and the customer has the right to inspect the accounts of the service provider to validate the level of profit.

- Having common or aligned strategies, for instance, in terms of growth, geography and technology areas.

- Having a similar size and culture in each organisation. If the managed service provider is an order of magnitude larger than the customer, then the focus on each customer is likely to be significantly less than it would be if they were more closely sized. Culture is harder to characterise, but it's easy to see cultural misalignments.

- Operating with shared risk/reward. A service provider is simply not going to offer improvements in performance or price unilaterally unless they have some incentive so to do. This means structuring the contract in a way that encourages innovation by the managed service provider for a share in the benefits.

As mentioned in the introduction to this book, in a managed service environment the role of SLM might be referred to as SDM or account manager. In this situation, and in a true partnership, the responsibility for promoting proactive improvements will therefore be the responsibility of the SDM or the equivalent role within the managed service provider.

PROACTIVE MANAGEMENT AND PREVENTION OF SERVICE RISKS

One of the characteristics that distinguishes more mature IT departments is the extent to which they operate proactively. One of the ways to do so is to help identify and proactively manage potential risks to customer services. In this respect, you are likely to be interfacing with your service owner/ manager colleagues. The value of your role is to recognise the importance of key services and the impact on the business of their loss or deterioration.

Similarly, you will be working together with process owner/ manager colleagues in problem management, availability management and capacity management, as well as with those responsible for CSI, to find proactive ways to improve the processes and procedures that underpin service delivery by providing control and consistency.

The challenge in less mature organisations is one of committing resources to proactive improvement. IT departments that work predominantly reactively will always be complaining about having insufficient time/people/money to be able to proactively improve services. Another characteristic of the reactive IT department is the 'hero culture'. In this environment, those who react to incidents by providing support during the small hours or at weekends are recognised and rewarded for it while those who spend time and effort managing projects and changes well enough to prevent incidents from happening in the first place are considered to be simply doing their job.

In this case, a cultural change is needed, and one way to start changing a reactive culture is to make the costs of this approach more visible. There are four costs associated with incidents but, perhaps surprisingly, these may not even be measured, let alone reported or used as the basis of proactive management.

The first and lowest cost is the internal rework necessary to deal with incidents and problems. This is represented by the time spent by anyone in second and subsequent line support handling incidents or problems assigned to them. When we ask about this, the most common response is in the 80–85 per cent bracket, and it is rare that we hear of values less than 30 per cent.

To calculate this reactive cost, apply this simple equation:

Average % of time spent on incidents/problems × number of people in second + line support × average fully loaded employment cost

This can be a surprisingly large figure, running into hundreds of thousands of pounds a year for a medium to large IT department.

The second lowest cost is the cost of the lost user time resulting from service unavailability. To calculate this cost, the service desk needs to record the number of users affected by incidents.

This is not necessary for all incidents, as incident priority in most IT departments is a factor of the number of users affected, such that only the highest two levels of priority affect multiple users. The calculation of lost user time is therefore:

Number of incidents × number of users affected × duration × average fully loaded user employment cost

You will need to take a view on the extent to which users are actually affected since, in some cases, the loss of a service may not prevent a user continuing to work or only partially affect their productivity. Nonetheless, this figure can run into millions of pounds per year for a medium to large organisation.

The third lowest (or second highest) cost is the impact of lost user time, or the opportunity cost. This is the commercial impact of users being unable to work or being partially affected by IT incidents. Implicitly, this is a higher cost than the lost user time itself since, at least in a commercial organisation, users would not be employed to generate less revenue than they cost. This is harder to measure but should be attempted, as it can be huge.

Finally, the most significant cost of IT incidents is the reputational damage to the company. Two obvious examples in recent times include the incidents suffered by Royal Bank of Scotland and Blackberry, both of which resulted in massive reputational damage, the latter unfortunately coinciding with the launch of the Apple iPhone.

Identifying and measuring the cost of incidents is one of the most effective ways to justify investing in proactive, preventative measures that will pay for themselves many times over. As SLM, you are in a position to help collect the relevant information and promote such an approach.

VALIDATING SUPPLIER CONTRACTS FOR CONTINUED ALIGNMENT WITH BUSINESS REQUIREMENTS

While contracts with suppliers are ideally established in the service design phase of the service life cycle, the alignment between these contracts and customer SLAs is an ongoing requirement in service operation. Validation of the alignment could usefully be done annually as part of the regular service level review process. It could also be triggered by the take-on of a new supplier, the renegotiation of a contract with an existing supplier or the establishment of a new or changed service level.

In all of these cases, you will have a key role to play together with the supplier manager, since you share the responsibility for ensuring that contracts with third parties align with and support the SLAs you have negotiated with your customers.

PROVIDING A POINT OF CUSTOMER CONTACT

On a day-to-day basis, you are one of the key interfaces between the business community and the IT department. Part of your role is therefore to make yourself available as a point of contact for the customers you represent and your colleagues in IT. This is not simply a reactive role but it also allows you to proactively provide relevant information, for instance about incidents, the early closure of a service or system and upcoming changes and their impact. The more active you are in this role, the more likely you are, in turn, to be kept informed, creating a virtuous circle.

With regard to incidents, it is important that you ensure that in the event of a major incident affecting any of the services or customers for which you are responsible, the service desk and/or incident manager informs you of the circumstances, the impact and what is being done to manage the incident, so that you can convey this to your customers.

MANAGING CUSTOMER REVIEW MEETINGS

This is one of the core activities of your role. Indeed, much of your time will either be spent at or preparing for these meetings. The importance of these meetings is hard to overstate. For your opposite number, these meetings are their primary interface with IT and will therefore form the basis of their relationship with IT and their opinion of IT.

The frequency of meetings is entirely at the discretion of you and your customers. Probably the most common frequency is monthly, but for more important services and customers there might be a weekly update or briefing, perhaps on a conference call where you might be joined by key people such as the incident and problem managers. If the interval between meetings is too long, say, six months, there is a risk that SLAs will become shelfware, and any relationships you have cultivated are likely to deteriorate.

As SLM, you are an IT ambassador, and to your customers you are representing IT. The key impression you should cultivate for these relationships is one of professionalism. This involves everything from attending the meetings on time, looking the part and being fully prepared to become a trusted partner by making and keeping appropriate commitments.

It is vital to understand the level of authority you have in the role. You need to be able to influence the provision of IT services around the SLAs and you need to have the authority to speak with your counterparts on behalf of IT. Without this authority, your customers will bypass you to get things done.

Having said that, a key mistake to avoid is overstretching your authority. The confidence and trust that your customers have in you and IT is easily destroyed by making commitments or promises that are outside the scope of your authority and that you may therefore not be able to deliver. Once trust has been lost in a relationship it is very hard, and takes a long time, to restore.

Planning and preparation

(See also Chapter 11 for additional information on customer review meetings.)

The service review meetings are a key interface between the IT department and the business, and in fulfilling the role of SLM, you are managing this interface on behalf of both parties.

In terms of preparation, there is nothing truer than the old saying, 'If you fail to plan, you plan to fail.' Planning is the key to a successful meeting. This means asking your customer what items they'd like to include on the agenda and agreeing it in good time beforehand. Ensure you review the minutes of the previous meeting, recognise any action points assigned to you and be prepared to respond to these, either by demonstrating that you have completed them or by describing progress with good reasons why you have yet to complete any actions that are beyond the agreed date.

A draft agenda is offered below.

1. Minutes of previous meeting and review of outstanding actions
2. Review of performance achieved against SLAs since last meeting
3. Explanation of missed service levels and the causes, performance variations and preventative actions
4. Review of business changes and plans for the next 3–12 months
5. Review of IT plans for the next 3–12 months
6. Agreement of actions
7. Any other business
8. Date of next meeting

The core of your discussions will focus on the performance of the services provided, tasks and actions undertaken by IT since your previous meeting, and, in particular, where any of these have failed to meet the service level or the reasonable expectation of your customer. Therefore, you essentially need two pieces of information at your finger tips: statistics and measurements demonstrating the extent to which IT met the service levels and expectations; and explanations for any situation that caused a service level or expectation to fail, ideally together with the action IT is taking to prevent any recurrence.

The basic principle is that any service levels and commitments made by IT to a customer have to be measured and reported. If you think about it, this is obvious, since making a commitment that can't be measured is somewhat pointless.

We will look at measuring and reporting performance shortly.

After the meeting

Following the meeting, it is good practice to send the minutes to the customer representative(s) with whom you met, and to anyone else you agreed should receive a copy. This might include, for instance, anyone referenced in the meeting but not present, anyone with an action, and your CSI manager, since there may be reference to a potential improvement.

As the IT representative, you have the responsibility of following up on your customer's behalf any agreed IT actions and progressing these with the relevant people within IT. My advice would be to maintain a single point of contact wherever appropriate and, rather than expecting your colleagues to follow up with your customer, have your colleagues update you so that you, in turn, can update your customer.

MEASURING AND REPORTING SERVICE PERFORMANCE

While all SLA commitments have to be measurable and have to be reported, it should not be your responsibility as the SLM to measure the activities to which IT is committing but the functional managers responsible for the operational activities. We referenced this in 'Reporting performance' above. This can be one of the biggest challenges you face in your role as SLM; first, because other managers may see it as your role, and second, because even if they recognise it as their responsibility, it still means that you are reliant on their activities to fulfil yours. The simple fact is that each function has responsibility not only for fulfilling their operational objectives but also for measuring them as the basis of effective management and CSI.

Your role is to gather and collate these operational measures into a consolidated report for your customer(s). This is not always as simple as it sounds. For instance, you will want a report of incidents by customer and/or service, yet the statistics provided by the incident management team may be produced and sequenced by priority or category. Furthermore, incident reporting might be spread across the incident management teams with no overall coordination.

Clearly, a good tool can facilitate reporting. Ideally, there is 'One source of the truth and multiple views.' In other words, the source of all statistics and reports should be one place, and the obvious place is the service management toolset. Furthermore, the more automation you can introduce to the reporting, the easier and quicker it is to produce reports, the greater the analysis potential, and there are likely to be fewer errors. However, toolset configuration is another dependency for you as SLM, as it is unlikely to be your responsibility or that you will have the necessary skills. Please see Chapter 7 for more information on tools.

If you are reliant to any extent on colleagues to produce information, you may obviously meet some resistance in obtaining that information since you have no line authority over them, and they will be under their own time pressures. There is no simple solution to this; essentially the entire IT team needs to buy into this way of working and accept their shared responsibilities.

Ideally, the information sources related to measuring performance are identified before the SLA is signed or the commitment made. Nonetheless, the challenge many organisations face is that performance is often not reported at a customer or business unit level.

The ideal reports comprise a blend of charts, tables and narrative. Charts are ideal for showing trends and allowing the reader to determine whether performance is improving, deteriorating or staying the same. However, there are some people, including those who work in finance, who have a strong scepticism of graphs, not least because they are often distorted to highlight variances. One example of this is a chart where the y-axis does not start at zero and which may therefore misrepresent the data.

To avoid any potential misunderstanding, charts should be accompanied by the same data in tabular form to allow the reader to make their own interpretation from objective data.

Generally speaking, by far the most useful aspect of a report is the narrative, since this provides the interpretation of the data and charts for the reader's benefit. The narrative allows the reader to understand the key messages of the report quickly and without ambiguity. Furthermore, each reader receives the same message.

Producing the narrative is your responsibility, although the key elements of it will hopefully have come from teams such as incident management, problem management and availability management. Essentially, any variance from normal should have an explanation. This might be a missed service level or simply an unusual value outside the normal range of values.

In many cases, you will not know the cause of the variation but will need to gather information from the relevant technical teams or the incident log. Once you have determined the cause, and if this is something undesirable, such as an incident, you should also understand what (if anything) is being done to prevent further recurrences. All of this information is of potential value to the reader and should therefore be included in the report, using appropriate language.

Another potential source of information is the service owners; they can contribute meaningful information from a service perspective.

The data in a typical report might look similar to Figure 5.1, a real, but anonymised, example to which the charts and narrative should be added.

Other activities you might wish to add to the report for your readers' benefit could include:

Figure 5.1 Sample weekly incident, problem and change activity report

Incident Management

Incident Summary

- All incidents reported upon logged between x[th] to xx[th] December yyyy

Environment	New Incidents Raised	Outstanding Incidents from Previous Weeks	Total Incidents Resolved	Total Incidents Outstanding
Production	3	1	4	
Pre-production	2			2
Disaster Recovery				
Production Support QA				
Production Support Development		1	1	
Project Support QA	1			1
Project Support Dev				
Training				
Environment Unspecified	3	2	2	3
Totals	9	4	7	6

	Number of Incidents	Met SLA	Failed SLA
Priority 1 - Critical	1	1	
Priority 2 - Major	2	1	1

P2 Failed Incident - INC 26648 1682497

Calls Outstanding by Age

- 1678386 Raised 6/12 Service Request
- 1678391 Raised 6/12 Service Request
- 1678398 Raised 6/12 SAP Service Terminating (Project Support QA)
- 1679627 Raised 8/12 Service Request
- 1681727 Raised 10/12 Originally P1, re-opened as P3. Service restored within 30 minutes to Pre-Production Cluster. PSOLPR3DBMS01 not available. Draft Incident Report issues 11/12 (INC 26572)
- 1682497 Raised 11/12 Unable to log onto servers VSOLPR4APPS01 & VSOLPR4APPS03. Service restored to all servers by 12:13 and within the SLA, with the exception of PSOLPR3APPS01 which was restored at 15:48. Awaiting confirmation (INC 26648)

Change Management

- All change activity reported to xth to xx[th] December yyyy

Change Management Summary

Changes Open	Changes Closed
14	9

	Closed Successfully	Closed Unsuccessfully	Cancelled	Rejected
Changes Closed	8	1	0	0

Problem Management

- All problem activity reported to xx[th] December yyyy

Problem Management Summary

Environment / Service	Ongoing Problems	New Problems Raised	Total Problems Resolved	Problems Outstanding
Environment Independent	1		1	
Production Support QA				
Pre Production	3	1		4
Production	1			1
Project Support QA				
DR & Training	3		1	2
Totals	8	1	2	7

- the change schedule;
- the projected service outage;
- planned maintenance periods;
- the schedule of continuity/disaster recovery tests.

Once you have defined a report structure, ideally this should be maintained from week to week or month to month so that the recipients will become familiar with it and find it easier to navigate through the report.

DATA GRANULARITY

When compiling performance reports, you need to recognise that the longer the measurement interval, the easier it is to achieve a defined level of performance. For instance, if the performance measure is 'Percentage of incidents resolved within service level, by priority', then this is easier to achieve measured over a monthly interval than a weekly interval.

USING MEANINGFUL MEASUREMENTS

One of IT's classic mistakes is to use measurements more relevant from an internal, technical perspective than from a customer perspective. Examples include the following.

- Defining availability in terms of percentage: typically, we include in an SLA a figure such as '99 per cent availability of the service'. To a customer, a far more meaningful measure is the number of minutes' downtime per week that this level of availability actually means.

- '95 per cent of priority 1 incidents will be fixed within 4 hours': while on the face of it this sounds reasonable, when there are only three or four priority 1 incidents in a month, what possible meaning can 95 per cent of these have?

- 'Transaction response time will be less than one second measured at the host': making a commitment to a customer about response time at the host is irrelevant. If the network delay adds another second to the response time, the sender will perceive a response time of up to two seconds and have no control over or recognition of the measure from the service providers' perspective.

Figure 5.2 Sample chart showing the number of respondents who selected each option

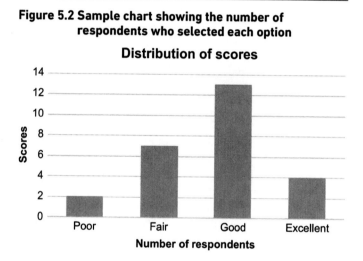

Another classic mistake in the use of measurements is to average customer satisfaction values by summing up the total values and dividing by the number of respondents. It is almost impossible to influence this figure. Far better is to report the number or percentage of respondents who gave each of the possible scores, as shown in Figure 5.2.

As ever, the trick is to think about performance from your customer's or stakeholders' perspective.

MANAGING REQUESTS FOR CHANGE

There will be occasions when your customer requests some form of change or variation to the service, perhaps on a temporary basis, but occasionally on a permanent basis. It is unlikely that you will have sufficient authority to make commitments to your customers on behalf of IT, so a key part of your role is to listen and understand not only the request but also the justification for and reasoning behind the request. From this information, you can help your customer build a business case for the change, if this is needed.

There are a number of processes and therefore, by implication, a number of roles with which you might interface in respect of a customer change request. Some of these will be influential in approving or managing the change, others may need to be kept informed. These roles may include:

- the service portfolio manager;
- the BRM;
- the CSI (or quality) manager;
- the service owner/manager;
- the business analyst.

    Your role in supporting the change request is to be your customer's single point of contact for it. This means gathering, understanding and conveying the request and keeping the customer informed of progress. In this situation, you are the 'voice of the customer' within the IT department, a pivotal role in ensuring requests are appropriately managed.

ACTING AS AN OUTBOUND COMMUNICATION CHANNEL

Not only does your role provide a voice for your customers within IT, it also provides a voice for IT out to the business. You therefore represent a channel for information to flow both ways, but yours is not the only channel. Other channels or interfaces might include those from:

- business relationship management;

- capacity management;
- financial management;
- the service desk;
- desk-side engineers/on-site technical support.

In addition, there are electronic communication channels, such as the intranet, the self-help portal, incident records and perhaps even newsletters.

A key requirement for supporting a professional approach to relationship management is ensuring that communications between IT as the service provider and business stakeholders are accurate, timely, meaningful and consistent. The list above shows that there are likely to be a multitude of interfaces and communication channels; ideally the service provider should manage these through a communication plan. It would be entirely appropriate if this plan were part of your responsibility. Alternatively, if it is owned by another role, it is essential that you are aware of and contribute to the plan as a key stakeholder.

The service provider's communication plan helps to ensure consistent and timely communication both within the IT department and between IT and its stakeholders. As such, it is likely to be referenced within OLAs and third party contracts, the former falling within your remit.

6 STANDARDS AND FRAMEWORKS

This chapter looks at the role of the SLM within related service management standards and frameworks, specifically the ISO/IEC 20000 standard and the ITIL and Control Objectives for Information and Related Technologies (COBIT) frameworks.

STANDARDS

Service level management is one of the processes within the scope of ISO/IEC 20000. The statements below that come from the standard are related to service level management. Since the standard encapsulates the essence of good service management practice that an auditor will verify is in place, by definition these practices are both generic and offer a list of primary objectives for each organisation.

The statements should not be considered exhaustive but rather represent a maturity level for the service level management process of between two (repeatable) and three (defined) on the process maturity scale (see Chapter 10). By implication, therefore, being able to meet the requirements of the standard will ensure that your organisation has a level of basic control over the process.

As SLM, you are responsible (together with the service level management process owner, should this role exist) for establishing and maintaining these practices.

Service level management

Text enclosed in quote marks is taken directly from the ISO/IEC 20000-2:2012 standard, with permission.

- 'The service provider shall agree the services to be delivered with the customer.'
  This is satisfied through the creation of SLAs.

- 'The service provider shall agree a catalogue of services with the customer.'
  This is addressed through production of the service catalogue.

- 'The catalogue of services shall include the dependencies between services and service components.'
  This is drawn from information contained both within the service catalogue and the configuration management system.

- 'For services delivered, one or more SLAs shall be agreed with the customer.'
  An obvious requirement, but recognising that each party's commitments are included, not just the service provider's.

- 'When creating SLAs, the service provider shall take into consideration the service requirements.'
  This is achieved by documenting the customers' service level requirements and showing how these relate to or form the basis of the SLAs.

- 'SLAs shall include agreed service targets, workload characteristics and exceptions.'
  The targets are by preference referred to as the service levels. The workload characteristics reference the volume, duration and arrival rate of customer demand. The exceptions identify any agreed exclusions (such as bank holidays). This also references any variations associated with the continuity plan, such as reduced service levels.

- 'The service provider shall review services and SLAs with the customer, at planned intervals.'
  This requires meetings to be arranged both regularly to review the service provision and typically annually to review the SLA. Meetings require an agenda and minutes to provide an audit trail, for instance when agreeing service improvement plans to address missed service levels. The meeting interval is set by agreement between the customer and supplier.

- 'Changes to the service requirements, catalogue of services, SLAs and other documented agreements shall be controlled by the change management process.'
  In other words, the service level requirements, service catalogue, SLAs and (for instance) underpinning contracts (UCs) are recorded as configuration items and managed (i.e. version-controlled, etc.) under the control of change management such that changes are assessed and recorded.

- 'The catalogue of services shall be maintained following changes to services and SLAs to ensure that they are aligned.'
  This is typically the role of the relevant service owner together with the SLM and the service catalogue manager.

- 'The service provider shall monitor trends and performance against service targets at planned intervals.'
  Clearly it is a basic tenet that any service level commitments should be measured and reported. In addition, changes over time (trends) should be identified.

- 'Results shall be recorded and reviewed to identify the causes of nonconformities and opportunities for improvement.'
  This is where service level management, which reports performance variations, interfaces with incident and problem management to drive CSI.

- 'For service components provided by an internal group or the customer, the service provider shall develop, agree, review and maintain a documented agreement to define the activities and interfaces between the two parties.'
  This references OLAs with the internal supply chain that underpin the SLAs.

- 'The service provider shall monitor performance of the internal group or the customer against agreed service targets and other agreed commitments, at planned intervals.'
  As for SLAs, OLA performance should be measured.

- 'Results shall be recorded and reviewed to identify causes of nonconformities and opportunities for improvement.'
  As for SLAs, this references the use of OLAs and OLA reporting to drive CSI.

Service reporting

Text enclosed by quote marks is taken directly from ISO/IEC 20000-2:2012, with permission.

- 'The description of each service report, including its identity, purpose, audience, frequency and details of the data source(s), shall be agreed between the service provider and interested parties.'
  This clause requires the service provider to define and record the relevant report information and the source of data from which the report is compiled. This is addressed by having each report defined as a configuration item and the source data identified within the configuration management system. 'Interested parties' includes any or all stakeholders of a service.

- 'Service reports shall be produced for services using information from the delivery of services and the SMS [service management system] activities, including the service management processes.'

In other words, all relevant activities contribute to the content of the service reports.

- 'Service reporting shall include at least:
  - performance against service targets;
  - relevant information about significant events including at least major incidents, deployment of new or changed services and the service continuity plan being invoked;
  - workload characteristics including volumes and periodic changes in workload;
  - detected nonconformities against the requirements in this part of ISO/IEC 20000, the SMS requirements or the service requirements and their identified causes;
  - trend information;
  - customer satisfaction measurements, service complaints and results of the analysis of satisfaction measurements and complaints.'

This is an unusually prescriptive list that echoes many of the requirements defined in service level management and can be used by the SLM as a menu of leading practice for the service report contents.

- 'The service provider shall make decisions and take actions based on the findings in service reports.'
  This may be an obvious statement; but this also needs to be demonstrated, for example through a documented audit trail from, for instance, exceptions or service level breaches through the service improvement plan to CSI.

- 'The agreed actions shall be communicated to interested parties.'
  This requires you to provide documentary evidence that improvement actions have been communicated to all relevant stakeholders, which will include those both within and outside the service provider organisation.

BEST PRACTICE FRAMEWORKS

Both the ITIL and COBIT frameworks reference service level management. Although both frameworks recognise the process as having both a proactive and a reactive responsibility, ITIL references it as a design process, but COBIT as a delivery and support process.

At a high level, the basic difference between the two frameworks (albeit one that is being eroded) is that ITIL describes the 'what' whereas COBIT describes the 'how'. Clearly this is a massive simplification, but ITIL regards itself as a source of generic good practice and therefore, by implication, tends to be less prescriptive, allowing the guidance to be adopted by organisations of any size, industry sector, geographic spread or technology focus. On the other hand, COBIT contains guidance on the actual adoption of good practice and has the objective of providing an auditable framework. ITIL starts to touch on this but only via the complementary guidance contained in, for instance, white papers and case studies available via the Axelos website.

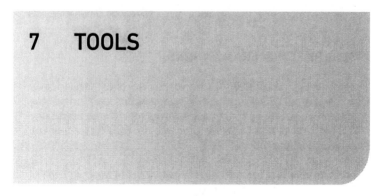

7 TOOLS

The tool most relevant to your role as SLM is your organisation's service management tool, as this chapter explains.

YOUR SERVICE MANAGEMENT TOOL

Your organisation's service management tool is used to log incidents, service requests, problems and changes. It may also log or interface with the tool(s) that contain(s) the service asset and configuration information, and log(s) events.[5]

Most of today's toolsets have fully integrated capabilities and provide extensive reporting that is usually customisable. It is this tool and its reporting capabilities that are critical to your role in that it is the source of information about workload volumes and performance. It is therefore also the source of the information that will allow you to determine the extent to which your organisation is meeting its service levels.

As we have already mentioned, these tools or toolsets typically report activities by type, such as incidents, or problems by priority. Your challenge is to gain a different perspective or view, namely one that represents customers or services. The ability to obtain this information will depend on two things: the extent to which this is possible in the toolset; and the ability (and willingness) of those responsible to enter the appropriate data accurately.

---

[5] Examples of such tools include Remedyforce and those offered by ServiceNow.

Regarding the second point, to report by service and/or customer requires the service and/or customer to be identified by the analyst and accurately logged in the record. To do this requires a definition of services and customers to be available to or configured within the tool and kept up to date, a task with which you might help, particularly if there is no service catalogue in place.

Essentially, you will need to be able to report performance against service levels both by service and customer for incidents, service requests, problems and changes as a minimum. This will be very time-consuming if not done automatically by the tool, but the tool is only capable of reporting using the appropriate parameters, and if the necessary information is entered.

You will need to verify the capability of the tool in this respect prior to commencing service level discussions with your customers. You will also need to ensure that the analysts responsible for creating and updating the records do so in the required way to support the analysis.

It would be hard to overestimate the importance of the tool capabilities and analyst activities in recording information, since this is the primary source of service level reporting. If the source information is available and accurate, then taking this data and building them into a report will depend on the extent to which the tool can do this, and/or on your own abilities. Even then, you still need to gather and report on exceptions and variances that will require potentially deeper analysis of the data and/or consultation with your colleagues.

Should your organisation have a disparate set of tools or tools that lack integration capability, then you may have to extract data separately from:

- the configuration management system/databases, in order to validate equipment type, locations and ownership (for instance);

- the event management system, to validate performance against service levels by tracking response time (for instance);

- the change management toolset, to report on the number and success of changes as well as the schedule of change and projected service outage report to advise your customers of upcoming events of relevance.

Ultimately, if the data you need is unavailable for whatever reason, then you either have to accept the situation or find a way to tailor the systems to be able to report the required information.

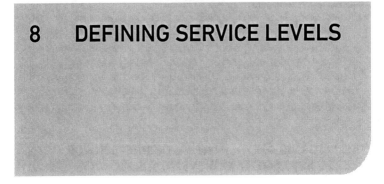

8 DEFINING SERVICE LEVELS

There are three important points to consider when dealing with defining service levels, and these are covered in this chapter.

Without doubt, defining service levels is a major responsibility for an SLM and one that can cause immeasurable difficulties if not considered carefully.

There is often pressure to define all service levels as soon as possible with a view to getting everything 'sorted out' at the first attempt. As you would expect, this in itself is usually a mistake that can lead to further mistakes and a situation akin to a world record attempt at domino toppling.

In addition, many SLMs feel the pressure to offer and agree service levels that will be seen to satisfy the customer. Thus, the language in the agreement can become very ambiguous and potentially dangerous; impossible service levels may be set unintentionally and the delivery of service and service achievements are then measured against them. As you can imagine, customers expecting a service that consistently meets (or beats) agreed service levels will be underwhelmed by the service provider's failure to meet them.

For example, many SLMs define an availability level for services as 99.99 per cent or a 'five 9s' figure, without any clear understanding of what this means, how it can be measured or how to achieve it. If the IT organisation reports that they have met their service levels on the basis of such a figure, even though the customer considers the service less than satisfactory, it can lead to customer dissatisfaction. Bad feeling emerges and what started as an exercise in building strong provider/customer relationships descends into a vicious cycle of blame and acrimony. This, in turn, may lead to other difficulties – reduced funding, cancellation of projects and other such evils. So, what should be done to avoid this?

MONITORING AND REPORTING OF PRE-SERVICE LEVEL AGREEMENT ACHIEVEMENTS

Avoid including anything in an SLA that cannot be effectively monitored and measured at a commonly agreed point. This is very important as inclusion of items that are difficult to monitor almost always results in disputes and eventual loss of faith in the service level management process.

In advance of, or in parallel with, the drafting of SLAs, review and upgrade existing monitoring capabilities in order to ensure that monitoring can be used to assist with the validation of proposed service levels during the service transition stage.

Monitoring must match the customer's perception of the service. Monitoring of individual components, such as the network or server, does not guarantee that the service will be available so far as the customer is concerned. Although a failure may affect more than one service, the customer's only concern is often the service they cannot access at the time of the reported incident.

Without monitoring all components of the end-to-end service (which may be very expensive) a true picture cannot be gained. Customers should report issues immediately so that the service provider is aware that service levels are being breached.

It is essential to ensure that any issue-handling service levels included in SLAs are the same as those included in any service desk tools and as those used for escalation and monitoring purposes. If you fail to recognise this and perhaps use defaults provided by the tool supplier, the tool may end up monitoring something other than that which has been agreed in the SLAs and therefore may be unable to show whether or not service levels have been met. Some amendments or modification may need to be made to the support tools, for example including the necessary fields to capture relevant data.

ENSURING SERVICE LEVELS ARE ACHIEVABLE BEFORE COMMITTING TO THEM

Most IT organisations use SLAs to document availability and other service levels that they have agreed with the business. It is important that these are negotiated and agreed by both sides. They need to be expressed in terms that are easy for the customer to understand and that can be measured and reported.

You may well be familiar with the helpful acronym for ensuring that service levels in SLAs are well written: SMART.

SMART service levels are defined in Table 8.1.

Table 8.1 SMART service levels

S	Specific	Service levels should be straightforward and emphasise what you want to happen.
M	Measurable	If a service level cannot be measured, then you cannot determine whether it has been achieved.
A	Achievable	It must be possible to achieve the service level with an acceptable investment of time and resources.
R	Relevant	Achieving the service level must contribute to the overall business mission.
T	Timely	The service level must be something that can be achieved and measured over the reporting period of the SLA.

What you should remember, however, is that while many organisations are good at measuring the availability and behaviour of infrastructure components, setting service levels based on these measurements does not necessarily provide any benefit to the business customer or user, who will typically only be interested in the end-to-end availability of the service to the users.

A traditional formula for measuring availability is:

$$Availability = \frac{AST - DT}{AST} \times 100\%$$

where AST is 'agreed service time' and DT is 'downtime'.

Simple – or is it? There are hidden dangers here if both AST and DT are only loosely described. It is all too easy for differences in views to hamper understanding and this, in turn, may lead to an ambiguous set of commitments. AST is relatively easy to agree and from the outset should be revisited on a regular basis to ensure that it does actually mean what it says. There will often be times when the service provider has to rejig their service offering to support their customers, meaning that the original AST is now compromised. The onus would be on you, the SLM, to review consistently how customers are using services in relation to set expectations and instigate the necessary reworking of SLAs as appropriate,

If AST is relatively easy to agree and set, DT is a potential nightmare. Is it referring to a loss of service that affects all users? Is the scope intended to include a partial failure only affecting one person? Does it include maintenance time? How do we actually measure DT? Does the customer have the ability to measure this in the same way you can? Do they need to?

You have probably asked or been asked these and many other questions while in the process of considering and building SLAs. There is, of course, no easy answer away from the hard work involved in building a strong relationship with the customer. It is to no good end that an SLM creates a service level (for example, availability of service), measured only from a provider perspective, and then presents what appears to be a compliant service at the review meeting. Imagine the scene:

SLM: 'Here's the report of service achievements for last week. All service levels met; you must be pleased.'

General looks of befuddlement and furrowed brows amongst all customer representatives present.

Customer: 'But the service was down all day last Tuesday...'

SLM: 'Never mind, we've still met our commitments.'

It would be better to agree in advance the criteria for measuring the service levels that can be accomplished by the service provider, no matter how high-level or simple they may be, review them and make changes as appropriate:

SLM: 'Here's the report of service achievements for last week. All service levels met; you must be pleased.'

General looks of befuddlement and furrowed brows amongst all customer representatives present.

Customer: 'Well, the commitments may have been met – but that includes the fact that the service was down all day Tuesday.'

SLM: 'OK then, let's discuss how we can make improvements...'

An altogether different conversation, you will agree.

We have concentrated largely on availability commitments, but this approach of test-and-review will work for other commitments, too – reliability, security, support, capacity, throughput, response times and continuity. Service levels can be measured by both parties – and it must be stressed that both parties have a responsibility to do this – and create a base understanding to build on. I am not advocating changing service levels all the time; this would prove to be counterproductive. However, in the early life of an SLA, an approach of regular review and small changes on a frequent basis will provide long-term benefits for relationships and trust.

VERIFYING SERVICE LEVEL COMMITMENTS PRIOR TO AGREEMENT

You should take care when performing the activity of determining the initial commitments for eventual inclusion in an SLA. Representatives of all the other processes and functions, such as those working in incident management on incident levels, need to be consulted for their opinion on what commitments can be realistically achieved. If there is any doubt, provisional commitments should be included in a pilot SLA that is monitored and adjusted through its early life support period.

One approach is to involve customers from the outset by producing a draft SLA with potential performance commitments as well as management and operational requirements, as a starting point for more detailed and in-depth discussion. Take care not to go too far: if you appear to present the customer with a fait accompli, this may unnecessarily limit open and productive dialogue.

An SLM should always seek to ensure clarity by differentiating between a customer requirement and the specific service level associated with satisfying that requirement. A requirement relating to performance, for example, might be informally expressed by the customer as 'fast enough to support the volume of orders to be placed without failures or delays', while the service level negotiated to support this requirement will define specific, measurable response times and the conditions under which the commitment will be deemed to have been breached.

It is not always easy to draw out the true business requirements, as the business may not know what it wants – especially if it has not been asked previously. The SLM may need to help the customer to understand and define their needs, particularly in terms of capacity, security and availability. The customer may describe what they want or need, after which the service provider must investigate and present back to the customer what is possible, along with the associated costs and risks of available options. Of course this is often an iterative activity requiring several rounds of negotiations before a balance is struck between what is sought and what is achievable and affordable. This process may involve a redesign of the service solution each time requirements and associated service levels are revised.

9 MARKETING THE SERVICE LEVEL AGREEMENT

This chapter covers the importance of marketing the SLA and some common approaches that can be taken.

THE IMPORTANCE OF MARKETING THE SERVICE LEVEL AGREEMENT

Service providers are dependent on their internal support teams as well as on external partners or suppliers. The service provider cannot commit to meeting service levels unless their internal support teams' and suppliers' performance underpins these service levels. Underpinning contracts with external suppliers are mandatory, but many organisations have also recognised the benefits of having simple agreements with their internal support teams.

It is important that the service provider builds trust and respect with the business, especially with the key business contacts. As SLM, you will contribute to this by working closely with your key business contacts to agree and deliver service levels. As customers experience increasingly effective IT support, their trust in and respect for the service provider will increase. This in turn improves the ability of the customer and service provider to work together efficiently and effectively. Managing the relationship with the business and its representatives, as undertaken by both the BRM and the SLM, helps to enroll the support of the people best placed to promote continual service improvement.

Additionally, the provider needs to ensure that business customers and their users fully understand all the nuances of the SLA. This will include their rights and responsibilities as well as the benefits. You will need to adopt a marketing mindset and prepare an internal marketing strategy designed to deliver these messages.

Internal marketing is sometimes absent or poorly managed, often because of the lack of perceived need. In practice, the entire success of service level management is dependent to a significant extent on the ability of the organisation to see and accept the need for formalising the relationship between internal teams. This means identifying and promoting the benefits of the process, and the purpose and value of having service level agreements.

An important part of your role as SLM may be to either conduct internal marketing in this respect or support management's internal marketing. Both sides need to be convinced of the benefits of formalising their relationship in this way in order for them to commit to making it work.

From the customer perspective, an SLA with their IT service provider should instil a degree of confidence in them that the provider is keen to understand and deliver against their requirements and expectations. This in turn will provide them with a consistent, predictable and reliable service.

From the provider's perspective, what can be better than having a documented and agreed definition of the required services and service levels against which they have to deliver? Should this not inform just about everything that the provider undertakes? After all, if it isn't focused on meeting or improving services and service levels, why would they do it?

The other obvious benefit for the IT service provider is that the SLA recognises that customers have responsibilities, too. The SLA identifies these and protects the provider from unreasonable requests. For instance, how often does IT get asked to configure a new location for a department that is moving offices, with two days' notice, when the department has been planning the move for perhaps six months? Similarly, the IT department cannot give an open-ended commitment to maintain transaction response times for an infinite number of concurrent transactions.

Nonetheless, it is not unusual to find some nay-sayers in the organisation who will mention 'wooden dollars' when they talk about paying money to internal service providers. Of course, committing to specific service levels does not imply that any money changes hands; and some will see this as a retrograde step on the grounds that they will lose the flexibility they had in asking for (or demanding!) immediate actions.

Other customer functions may see the whole concept of documented internal agreements as an unnecessary overhead or documentation 'for the sake of it'. I have found that a very effective way of dealing with this attitude is to invite the doubters to participate in one of the service management simulation exercises offered by specialist organisations. This provides the opportunity to experience first-hand the challenges of managing service provision in an uncontrolled, undocumented environment and is universally effective at changing these often entrenched attitudes.

It is interesting to contrast the approach to IT service delivery between in-house teams and managed service providers. No-one questions the need for service level agreements as part of a contract with an external supplier. It may seem more appropriate in that context because money is changing hands and the SLA/contract provides a means of measuring and evaluating the service provider against defined criteria in order to agree penalties or credits.

So why should the governance of an internal supply model not be subject to the same good practice, simply because no money is changing hands? Having a clear and documented agreement of services and service levels to be provided, a shared understanding of good practice and the agreed commitments of each party to ensure the successful delivery of the service is surely good practice regardless of whether or not the IT service provider is part of the organisation.

I would be quite surprised if you as SLM did not come up against some of this negative thinking within your organisation. You should therefore be prepared to deal with it and be able to provide good reasons to justify managing service levels in this way.

Internal marketing is not a one-off activity but something that needs to be addressed at regular intervals, if not routinely. The review and management of service level agreements is an instance of this, as it ensures that the services covered and the service levels for each remain and continue to be seen as relevant and worthwhile.

MANAGEMENT SUPPORT

It would be negligent not to mention that although as an SLM you have a key role in developing and marketing SLAs and service levels both internally and externally, a CSF in having meaningful and effective SLAs is the active, ongoing and visible support of your colleagues, particularly the senior IT leadership team. Too often service levels become shelfware because they were established as part of an initiative or project rather than a permanent change in the way IT services are managed and delivered.

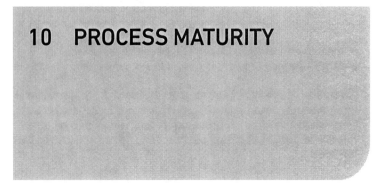

10 PROCESS MATURITY

The ITIL process maturity framework defines five levels of maturity, which are set out in this chapter along with the minimum requirements for an effective process maturity analysis.

PROCESS MATURITY LEVELS

The five levels of process maturity are:

- initial;
- repeatable;
- defined;
- managed;
- optimising.

While the maturity level appropriate for a process in an organisation is, to a large extent, dependent on the objectives and strategy of the organisation and the demands of its business, perceived wisdom is that 'defined' or Level 3 represents basic control and is therefore a pragmatic target.

Your role as SLM includes identifying the level of process maturity appropriate for your organisation and periodically evaluating it to validate its fitness for purpose. A process maturity analysis can make comparisons with the same process in other organisations, but this is of limited value; the analysis is better carried out against ITIL leading practice for the process.

PROCESS MATURITY ANALYSIS

The scope of an effective process maturity analysis specifically for the service level management process should include, as a minimum:

- the presence of a process owner and process manager(s);
- the existence and completeness of the process policy;
- the existence and completeness of process procedures;
- the degree of integration and effectiveness of the relationship with related processes, such as supplier management, business relationship management, incident management and service catalogue management;
- the existence and completeness of underpinning OLAs;
- the alignment of contractual obligations in supplier contracts and service levels contained within SLAs;
- the production, clarity, completeness and distribution of performance reports;
- the existence and effectiveness of service review meetings;
- the scope of the process in terms of the number of services and business units covered;
- the management of service improvement programmes;
- the effectiveness of complaint handling.

11 A DAY IN THE LIFE OF A SERVICE LEVEL MANAGER

The purpose of this chapter is to provide, for those either new to the role or considering taking on such a role, an insight into the typical working day and activities of an SLM. Clearly this will vary not only from day to day but also from organisation to organisation.

FIRST THINGS FIRST

Your first task of the day is to learn about any major incidents that occurred since you last checked. Even if these were managed within service levels, it is vital that you understand what happened, which parts of the business were affected and how.

If the customers affected by the incident(s) have not yet contacted you, you should contact them to appraise them of the circumstances, impact and remedial activities IT has completed or is undertaking. My preferred means for doing this would be the phone rather than email. However, if you can't reach the customer by telephone, leave a voicemail and send a text message with the incident number and brief details and ask them to call you. Customers dislike nothing more than being kept in the dark.

What you're trying to determine and communicate is the business impact of the incident(s) and the estimated time to restore the service.

Depending on how critical IT services are to your business, you may take an even more proactive approach by asking to be kept informed of major incidents outside office hours. You will want to avoid a situation where you learn about incidents from your customers before you do from your colleagues.

If major or significant incidents have occurred (typically the highest two levels of priority), it is likely that a significant proportion of your day is going to be focused on gaining an understanding from your IT colleagues about the incident(s) and communicating appropriately with your customers.

Hopefully this will not be typical of your day! You will instead be engaged somewhere in the cycle of gathering and reviewing performance reports, and meeting or otherwise engaging with your customers.

PERFORMANCE REPORTS AND SERVICE IMPROVEMENT

Assuming you have several customers, you already have SLAs in place with them and you meet with them perhaps on a monthly basis, most of your time between meetings is going to be spent preparing performance reports or working on service improvement programmes. As already indicated, it is not your responsibility to gather performance data; this is the role of the operational teams, such as the service desk, incident management and change teams as well as service owners. Instead, you should be gathering information from these teams and collating it into reports on a per-customer basis.

Obviously there will be some things to report that are of interest or relevance to all customers, but your opposite numbers will also appreciate regular reporting specifically relevant to their business unit, rather than simply a review of overall IT performance. If the systems and toolsets don't report by customer, this might need to be handcrafted by you.

Hopefully, much of the reporting will be automated, leaving you with the task of interpreting the statistics. From a customer perspective, the best reports comprise a combination of three aspects.

- Charts of performance against service levels – the value of charts is that they can clearly show trends.

- Tables of values used in the charts – it is a truism that some people (most notably those who work in finance) are sceptical of charts and prefer to see actual values. You therefore need to ensure that these are included in the reports.

- The most important part of any performance report is the interpretation of variances and, in particular, missed service levels.

The third of these aspects will make up the bulk of your daily activities and provide the focus for your customer meeting preparation. This can be an interesting part of your work. While your customers will obviously want to know how well IT has met their requirements, their main focus will be what caused service levels to be affected and what IT is doing to recover and prevent a recurrence of the situation.

To handle your customer meetings effectively, you will need to discuss with your IT colleagues the circumstances of IT's management of incidents, service requests and requests for change. Your objective is to provide full information to your customers to improve their confidence in and satisfaction with IT services.

A word of warning – never assume that statistics are correct, even those that are produced by the systems and toolsets. One of your key tasks is therefore to assure the accuracy of the data you will present to your customers to ensure their continued confidence in you and your reporting.

COMMUNICATION

Spending the majority of your time talking to your customers and in meetings with them is usually the best use of your time. Whether or not your organisation employs BRMs or account managers, your role will be instrumental in influencing your customer's perception of IT.

In my personal experience, the industry was shortsighted to remove the 'C' from what in the 1980s, with the integration of the network teams into IT, became 'ICT', where 'C' stands for 'Communications.' Sadly, the skill and activity most often in short supply in IT is communication. Your role as SLM is one of the key interfaces between the IT service provider and their customer and, along with the BRM, you should be knowledgeable about how IT technology can support business processes and activities. Part of your day-to-day role therefore should be to promote and contribute to effective communication.

For instance, one of the easy mistakes to make in this role is assume that the performance reports and statistics you present tell the full story. The best example of this is that on the hopefully not so rare occasion that IT meets all its service levels one month, you may be surprised to find out that your customers are not necessarily completely satisfied with the services provided. In many, if not most, cases this can be a consequence of inadequate or incomplete communication.

I can offer an example from personal experience. Having documented the SLA with the finance department and meeting the customer's service levels consistently over a period of time, I met with the finance director and asked if she was happy with the service. Confidently expecting a positive answer, I was slightly disappointed to hear, 'Yes, but...' The 'but' was qualified as follows.

'Once a month on a Friday night, you run a suite of batch jobs. If one of those fails, you have rerun procedures, but what you fail to realise is that one of those jobs produces the trial balance. This in turn produces a printout that you send to the head office where we have three people coming in at 09:00 on overtime in order to check the figures.'

'OK', I said, 'so what do you want me to do if the job fails?'

'Call me', she said.

'But it runs at 03:00 in the morning!'

'Nonetheless, call me, tell me the cause of the failure, what you're doing to restore the situation and when we can expect the printout to arrive.'

'And what will you do?'

'I'll call the three people I've booked to come in on overtime and let them know what time they should aim to arrive at head office, based on what you've told me. That way, they don't have to get out of bed so early on a Saturday morning and I don't have to pay them overtime to read the papers.'

For me, this was a telling insight. Too often in IT we hide behind the numbers and fail to recognise the business impact of what to us is simply a job failure. The learning point is that a key part of the role of the SLM is to understand IT services from a customer as well as an IT perspective. Examples like this serve to show that there can be serious disconnects between the two, and unless you understand your customer's perspective, you can't hope to build an effective relationship.

MEETING PREPARATION

It is an old but nevertheless true saying that 'Proper planning prevents poor performance.' The effectiveness of your customer meetings is, without question, a function of the completeness of your preparation. Good practice is to prepare and distribute an agenda ahead of the meeting, making sure that your customer has an opportunity to raise any specific agenda items of their own; this may influence who accompanies you to the meeting. It is also good practice to send a copy of the minutes of your previous meeting with the agenda.

Whether or not you send the actual performance reports to the customer before the meeting is questionable. My preference is to do so to allow your customer to review the results beforehand to make the most of the actual meeting time. If you choose this path, it is clearly essential that the reports are self-explanatory. We discussed the format of performance reports in 'Measuring and reporting service performance' in Chapter 5. Together with the charts and data tables, the key aspect of any report that makes it self-explanatory is the inclusion of a narrative to explain any unexpected variations or missed service levels.

Have a clear idea of what you want from the meeting in terms of outcomes. If there's something specific, make sure that you have done all you can to give yourself the best chance of achieving your objectives.

Please also refer to 'Managing customer review meetings' in Chapter 5.

AT THE MEETING

Customer meetings can be stressful but can also be the most satisfying part of the role. If you have properly and fully prepared for the meeting, it is an opportunity to understand what your customer thinks of the service they receive, and a chance to influence their perception positively and build an effective relationship based on trust.

Almost everything you do on a day-to-day basis should be focused on having successful discussions and meetings with your customers. Your customer's opinion of IT will be significantly influenced by their perception of the value of these meetings.

Recognise when you attend the meetings that you are representing their supplier, and that their opinion of IT will be influenced not only by the quality of the service they receive and the extent to which their requirements are being met, but it will also be influenced by how they perceive *you*. Although this is an internal meeting, my advice is to approach it as professionally as you would if your customer worked for another organisation. In other words, apply all the normal protocols you would when trying to win their business: arrive on time, dress appropriately, make sure you know the names and roles of the people who will be at the meeting and ensure you take along sufficient printed copies of the agenda and reports. If you intend to use a projector and/or flip chart or whiteboard, make sure beforehand that these will be available and take your own set of marker pens along.

These are not just niceties but give your customers confidence that you know your job and take your responsibilities seriously. You might also consider using some classic relationship management techniques, such as keeping notes about the lives of your customers outside work, their families, hobbies and interests. Not only can this help build an effective relationship, it supports their perception that you are genuinely interested and care about them.

None of this may come naturally to you, but the opportunity to practice and enhance these techniques in a 'friendly' environment, that is, with people in the same organisation, will stand you in good stead for future roles that interface with representatives from other organisations.

AFTER THE MEETING

Once you return to your desk, it is good practice to drop your customer a line to thank them for their time and summarise what you agreed at the meeting. If you took formal minutes, send these not only to your customer but also, as a matter of course, to anyone else referenced in the minutes as well as your manager. If there are any points about which you are unsure, there's no reason why you can't call or email your customer for clarification; better to be clear than to proceed on an invalid assumption.

You then need to decide which colleagues you need to engage to progress the action points assigned to you. If there is a timeline or deadline associated with these, good practice is to report progress and any issues before the deadline to keep your customer informed (it's truly remarkable how some service provider representatives keep bad news to themselves and fail to manage their customer's expectations, and then wonder why meetings are adversarial!).

INFLUENCING WITHOUT AUTHORITY

The ability to 'influence without authority' is a key skill necessary for the SLM (more on this in the next chapter). Your ability to do this successfully is a critical attribute of the role since, unless you are very senior within IT, there is little, if anything, you will have the authority to agree with your customers on behalf of IT. Instead you are in some ways acting as a go-between or message carrier. Even if you are a subject matter expert in the relevant field, it does not give you the required authority, although it may help you to strengthen the business case for a path of action.

To be successful requires a combination of understanding and practice. Given that someone outside your sphere of authority is not obliged to respond to your requests and can undoubtedly come up with many reasons why they can't or won't do so, how can you enlist their support and commitment?

One of the most effective ways I have found of winning people over while recognising their pressures and objectives is to discuss with them the wider department's objectives and the responsibilities you all share for making your department successful. Less subtly, you can engage their manager to win that person's mandate for their colleague's support.

SUMMARY

In summary, a typical day in the life of an SLM is focused on recognising, meeting, reporting and improving on the service provider's ability to meet the negotiated service levels.

This is probably the most important aspect of IT service provision, because the services and associated service levels represent the essence of what your customers need from IT and therefore the focus of everything that IT does. On a daily basis, you should therefore ensure that your colleagues recognise and support service level management and use it as the basis of CSI.

12 CAREER PROGRESSION AND SKILLS DEVELOPMENT

This chapter looks at the career development potential for the SLM both within and beyond the employer organisation.

CAREER PROGRESSION

The role of an SLM is an ideal springboard for furthering your career in IT. If you wish to develop your career within your current organisation, you have two choices: move higher up the management structure within IT, or move from an IT role to a business role. Alternatively, you have the option of gaining sufficient expertise in the role to be able to undertake it in another, perhaps larger, organisation or become an independent contractor or consultant, advising organisations on good practice in the field and supporting the achievement of their objectives.

Developing your career within your organisation

If you are looking to develop your career within your current organisation, the role of SLM will assist, whether you wish to progress within or outside IT. While many of your IT colleagues will have better-developed technical skills, the higher you rise in the management structure of IT, the less relevant become your technical skills and the more so your management skills.

An understanding of IT management comes naturally to SLMs because a significant proportion of your time will be spent in meetings and discussions with your opposite numbers in the business world. Their view of IT is often quite different from that of your IT colleagues. First, they may see IT as a tool or capability and a means to an end rather than an end in itself. Second, their impression of IT is formed from a limited perspective, namely their interaction with IT services and applications; their end-user device, be it a PC, personal digital assistant (PDA) or terminal; and the contacts they have with IT staff, usually you and the service desk. Once you recognise and empathise with the business perspective of IT, you start to appreciate the impact of IT on business operations, warts and all. This knowledge is a prerequisite to understanding how to improve IT services and the value that IT delivers.

If you carry this understanding into a higher IT management role, it will give you the ability to determine how IT can play an increasingly effective role in underpinning business processes and improving competitiveness, for instance. Typically, the higher up the IT management chain you progress, the closer the role becomes to a business role. Your time as an SLM will be invaluable in this respect.

Three roles in particular represent a natural progression for you as SLM within your own organisation:

- SDM – not to be confused with the role of the same name that typically represents the SLM in a managed service provider: rather this is the role that is responsible for the management and delivery of all live services within an internal service provider;
- quality or CSI manager;
- BRM.

These titles can be used in different ways in different organisations. SDMs are usually responsible for the infrastructure side of IT, their opposite number being the applications manager or equivalent. In smaller organisations, this role is likely to report to the chief information officer (CIO) or head of IT, but it will still be a relatively senior role in larger IT departments.

The role of quality manager or CSI manager is a very natural progression because both service level management and quality management focus on the value delivered by services rather than by technology. Figure 12.1 shows the relative perspectives of technology and services.

Figure 12.1 Relative perspectives of processes, services and technology

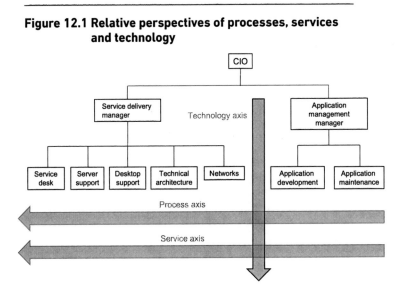

The technology axis is relevant because it represents people's skills and the classic organisational structure. However, services and service management processes, such as incident, problem and change management, operate in a different dimension, shown in Figure 12.1 as the horizontal axis because their focus is on underpinning and delivering business value from IT rather than managing the technology that 'keeps the lights on'.

The BRM role differs from the SLM role in three key ways:

- It engages with the most senior stakeholders in the organisation rather than with customer representatives (although in smaller organisations there is a potential for overlap).

- It maintains a strategic rather than a tactical perspective on IT, for instance how IT can support the business strategy and underpin areas such as expansion, acquisitions and divestments, and new markets and capabilities.

- It has a significantly longer planning horizon, typically one to five years rather than the 12–18 months usually associated with service level management.

Despite these differences the progression from SLM to BRM is a natural one because their skills and perspectives are very similar.

One thing to beware of though is that sometimes the role referred to as BRM is actually that of an account manager and carries a sales target. This puts an entirely different perspective on the role and requires different skills.

Other internal opportunities

Depending on how well established your IT department and how mature service management is, there may be other opportunities for you to take a leading role. These might include IT service continuity management, since your business colleagues will expect the services referenced in the SLA to be protected in the event of significant disruption and outages. You might also lead discussions into service costing, something remarkably few organisations even attempt. Another area might be end-to-end management of the supply chain, for example through a SIAM approach in an environment with multiple subcontractors. A key interface will be with the CSI or quality management team; if this function is immature or non-existent, this represents another opportunity for leadership, or even a specific career opportunity.

When an IT department is more accomplished at defining and meeting its business's objectives, it may consider aiming for the ISO/IEC 20000 standard to provide external validation of its alignment with good practice and conformance to standards. This is clearly an area of opportunity for you in which to either lead or influence. More information on the requirements of the standard in respect of service level management can be found under 'Service level management' in Chapter 6.

A business-based career

Should you consider a business-based career, your natural next step would be the role of business unit or departmental IT manager. Most organisations recognise the benefit of having an ex-IT person managing the IT within a business unit or department, and this represents a clear opportunity for someone with a background in and blend of IT and business skills.

Your understanding of IT and service delivery principles will make you a more informed buyer of IT services – not something that comes naturally to people with little or no IT experience. By 'speaking the same language' as your IT provider, you can have a more intelligent dialogue with their representatives, appreciate much of their technical perspective and better understand how IT can add value to business processes and activities.

Many organisations move managers from an IT to a business role for this reason and, indeed, I have seen this work effectively the other way around; the core principle being that this approach leads to greater understanding and cooperation between IT and business people and greater synergy between their activities.

Contracting and consulting

The potential of the SLM role as a springboard into the contracting or consultancy world is really a consequence of the many touch points of the role with other IT areas. These are described in 'Interfaces and dependencies' in Chapter 3.

In the contract world, quite simply, the broader your range of skills, the more likely you are to find work, since there are more areas in which you can be placed. One word of advice though: to be a successful contractor, you should ideally have worked for a number of organisations beforehand. It is more difficult to succeed in the contract world if you have only worked for one or two organisations, regardless for what length of time.

The skills and experience you gain as an SLM are undoubtedly a useful launchpad for consultancy. This is because you gain an understanding of the business/IT interface, services and service value, organisational structures, performance measurement and management, and all the complementary areas referenced in this guide. Successful consultants develop a broad but comprehensive understanding of how IT can add value to business activities and processes and use this experience to advise their clients.

SKILLS DEVELOPMENT

This section identifies and explores the skills typically useful to the role of SLM and thus provides a training needs analysis or skills matrix.

Management skills

In your role as SLM, you will have an opportunity to practise many of the skills associated with management. These typically include:

- leadership and collaboration skills;
- people management skills;
- communication skills;
- business management skills;
- financial skills;
- project management skills.

Leadership and collaboration skills

Leadership skills include a range of capabilities that span influencing and negotiation, building relationships, navigating politics and managing conflicts. Such skills are learnt and honed by:

- understanding how to manage people with differences in culture, working styles and business experience;
- creating clarity, building trust and optimising individual and team performance;
- leading virtual teams;
- building collaborative trust and helping people to focus on results;
- time and stress management for both you and your people;
- developing your personal influence and impact by navigating organisational politics and the 'informal' organisation to secure resources, collaborate and get things done;
- interacting with others to achieve results, for example by enhancing your working relationships to improve your business outcomes;
- negotiating effectively to deal with business situations and get better results in every negotiation.

While this is a generic set of leadership and collaboration skills, it is intriguing to note how relevant this is to your role as SLM. Therefore, your role provides you with the perfect opportunity to develop the key generic leadership and collaboration skills necessary to succeed in higher managerial roles.

If you are the first SLM in your organisation, you will implicitly be instrumental in leading the service level management process towards a higher level of maturity, or indeed developing it from scratch. Regardless of the fact that the process will likely have management and/or sponsorship from a more senior manager, they will usually be very happy to allow you significant discretion in the development of your role and the service level management process if you prove willing and capable.

The role of SLM offers as many interfaces across both IT and the business as any other IT role, if not more. In almost all your dealings with colleagues on both sides, you are unlikely to have any managerial authority over these colleagues. You will therefore have to develop the key skill of being able to 'influence without authority' through capabilities such as being diplomatic, insightful, persuasive, recognising all the dimensions of a debate by seeing other peoples' perspectives, building a convincing business case for a course of action and leading by example.

Unless you are or will be the IT signatory of SLAs, one of your primary roles is to gather the business's requirements and the related justification and, in effect, sponsor these within IT. This means liaising with IT colleagues in areas such as financial, technical, change, availability and capacity management and various other areas. You will have no authority over these colleagues, but by virtue of your role and your ability to present these requirements in a convincing and reasoned way, you will be attempting to influence the outcome in a positive way.

Again, if service level management is a new or relatively new concept within your organisation, a key requirement, and one that you might choose to lead, is to develop the performance management framework. Since measuring and reporting every SLA commitment is obligatory, it is essential that IT is aware of its capabilities before even discussing the business's service level requirements, otherwise, as discussed previously, there is a risk that IT as the service provider signs up to service levels that are as yet undeliverable. If the current performance management framework is inadequate or immature, you may opt to take a direct role in its development and so grow and strengthen your leadership qualities further.

People management skills

This area encompasses the ability to attract, retain, motivate, coach and develop team members for high performance. You may have limited opportunity to practise these skills if you are a 'one-person band', but in larger organisations with a team of SLMs there may be greater opportunity to practise them.

Communication skills

Your success as an SLM is critically underpinned by your ability to communicate in all directions: upwards with senior management and stakeholders; downwards with anyone working for you; and laterally with colleagues both in the business and in other areas of IT.

To be able to communicate effectively, you need to be able to frame your ideas in strategic business language, speak and understand the language of senior managers and make a professional impression. You also need to be able to interact with others to get things done.

Communication skills are so important in all walks of life that having the chance to practice and develop these as an integral part of your role is an invaluable learning opportunity that will stand you in good stead throughout your career.

Business management skills

Business management skills include understanding the core disciplines of general management and how different functions work together to implement the strategy, for instance by:

- creating more value;
- analysing opportunities, resources and risks;
- planning, organising and monitoring work to get things done and create value for your organisation.

Financial skills

Every manager requires basic financial skills such as understanding, interpreting and acting on financial information that contributes to business profitability, as well as drawing up realistic budgets, managing cash and delivering results.

Project management skills

Project management skills involve understanding the people side of projects and project planning to deliver within time and budget. A useful area of training that also provides a qualification in project management is PRojects IN a Controlled Environment (PRINCE2).

Job-related skills

Skills Framework for the Information Age

The Skills Framework for the Information Age (SFIA, www.sfia-online.org/en) provides guidance on the requirements of specific job roles in terms of the skills and skill levels required by the job holder. For the SLM, the core skills, listed below with their SFIA code and definition (enclosed in quote marks where it has been taken directly from the Framework, with permission) are usually considered to be:

- Service level management (SLMO): 'The planning, implementation, control, review and audit of service provision, to meet customer business requirements. This includes negotiation, implementation and monitoring of service level agreements, and the ongoing management of operational facilities to provide the agreed levels of service, seeking continually and proactively to improve service delivery and sustainability targets.'

- Relationship management (RLMT): The identification, analysis, management and monitoring of relationships with and between stakeholders. (The full definition for this skill in the SFIA is available at www.sfia-online.org.)

- Change management (CHMG): The management of change to the service infrastructure, including service assets, configuration items and associated documentation, be it via request for change (RFC), emergency changes, incidents or problems, providing effective control and treatment of risk to the availability, performance, security and compliance of the business services impacted. (The full definition for this skill in the SFIA is available at www.sfia-online.org.)

- Release and deployment (RELM): 'The management of the processes, systems and functions to package, build, test and deploy changes and updates (which are bounded as "releases") into a live environment, establishing or continuing the specified Service, to enable controlled and effective handover to Operations and the user community.'

- Problem management (PBMG): 'The resolution (both reactive and proactive) of problems throughout the information system lifecycle, including classification, prioritisation and initiation of action, documentation of root causes and implementation of remedies to prevent future incidents.'

Additional skills that are usually considered to contribute to the role are:

- IT infrastructure (ITOP): 'The operation and control of the IT infrastructure (typically hardware, software, data stored on various media, and all equipment within wide and local area networks) required to deliver and support IT services and products to meet the needs of a business. Includes preparation for new or changed services, operation of the change process, the maintenance of regulatory, legal and professional standards, the building and management of systems and components in virtualised computing environments and the monitoring of performance of systems and services in relation to their contribution to business performance, their security and their sustainability.'

- Incident management (USUP): 'The processing and coordination of appropriate and timely responses to incident reports, including channelling requests for help to appropriate functions for resolution, monitoring resolution activity, and keeping clients appraised of progress towards service restoration.'

- Sourcing (SORC): 'The provision of policy, internal standards and advice on the procurement or commissioning of externally supplied and internally developed products and services. The provision of commercial governance, conformance to legislation and assurance of information security. The implementation of compliant procurement processes, taking full account of the issues and imperatives of both the commissioning and supplier sides. The identification and management of suppliers to ensure successful delivery of products and services required by the business.'

Finally, an awareness of quality management is considered desirable:

- Quality Management (QUMG): 'The application of techniques for monitoring and improvement of quality to any aspect of a function or process. The achievement of, and maintenance of compliance to, national and international standards, as appropriate and to internal policies, including those relating to sustainability and security.'

APPENDIX A: SAMPLE SERVICE LEVEL AGREEMENT

We offer here a sample SLA that represents good service level management practice. It should be used as a guide rather than a template since each organisation is unique and, if used as a template, the sample may be either deficient or irrelevant in some areas.

SAMPLE SERVICE LEVEL AGREEMENT

Effective date:	

Document owner:	

Version

Version	Date	Revision/ description	Author

Approvals

Name	Role	Action	Date
		Approver	
		Approver	
		Reviewer	
		Reviewer	

Approver sign-off is to signify agreement or acceptance of the document. Reviewer sign-off is to signify that they have read the document. All other recipients need take no further action.

CONTENTS

1. GENERAL OVERVIEW

This is a service level agreement (SLA) between IT service delivery and the organisation (referred to here on in as the business) and is intended to provide a high-level overview of the service levels the business can expect from key IT services.

This SLA shall remain valid until revised or terminated and will document:

- the key IT services provided to the business;
- the general levels of response, availability and maintenance associated with these services;
- the responsibilities of IT service delivery and the business.

This SLA is underpinned by operating level agreements (OLAs) with internal support providers (e.g. internal IT support teams) and underpinning contracts (UCs) with external service providers.

The SLAs contained in this document will initially be monitored and adjusted quarterly. Any revisions to this document will be communicated to the review and sign-off personnel.

Thereafter, an annual review and sign-off of this document will take place to ensure the service levels are still relevant to meeting business requirements.

1.1 Services offered

This SLA will cover the following business services:

Service 1

Service 2

Service 3

Service 4

Other business applications:

Application 1

Application 2

Application 4

Application 5

Application 6

2. SERVICE AVAILABILITY AND SERVICE HOURS

Production gold and silver services will be available for use 24 hours a day, 7 days a week, excluding planned maintenance weekends, emergency maintenance or in the event of a major incident (i.e. an incident with either the highest priority or the highest impact). The service level standards are specific measurable characteristics of the service levels, such as availability, performance, resilience and response. Table 2.1 sets out the key characteristics of the three service level standards.

Table 2.1 Key characteristics of the service level standards

Service level standard	Availability (%) – excluding planned maintenance hours	Support hours	Disaster recovery + service continuity recovery time
Gold	99.0	24 x 7	Yes. N+ 12
Silver	98.0	24 x 7	No
Bronze	97.0	10 x 5 (8 a.m. – 6 p.m.)	No

Note: N = point in time at which disaster recovery is invoked. This will be after the diagnosis of an incident has been completed and assessed as representing a major incident.

2.1 Planned maintenance and service exceptions

Once a month, there may be an outage of up to six hours to allow for essential planned maintenance to be carried out on one or more services (or service components). This will usually be scheduled for the second weekend in the month, commencing at 9pm on Friday.

Dates will be published three months in advance and maintained on the change management schedule. For an up-to-date change management and maintenance schedule, please refer to the corporate intranet.

Planned maintenance is work that is approved by the IT CAB, and therefore this time is excluded from the availability calculation.

2.2 Emergency maintenance

To minimise business impact, IT service delivery will endeavour to complete emergency maintenance outside core service hours and provide as much notice as possible. However, if a situation is critical it may be necessary to interrupt availability of a service at short notice.

2.3 Peak business schedule

To minimise the risk to our production environment during peak business periods, changes requested through projects, requests or planned maintenance may not be permitted during the change freeze. Table 2.2 illustrates the peak business periods.

Table 2.2 Peak business periods

Period	Business reason
November, December and January	Peak trading, particularly post-Christmas
March and April	Finance very busy before and after financial year end

3. SERVICE LEVELS FOR HELP AND SUPPORT

3.1 Help and support available if you have an issue with the service

The IT service desk is the single point of contact for all IT-related incidents, and any IT-related incident that impacts a user's ability to use IT services should be reported to the IT service desk. Unless otherwise stated, the IT service desk is available 24 hours a day, 7 days a week. Please note that the level of resource on the service desk flexes in line with the business day, that is, there is a higher level of resource covering the hours of 8am to 6pm (UK time) Monday to Friday – these are referred to as 'core service hours'.

Contact details:

Phone: Internal: nnnn (DDI: nnnn nnn nnnn).
Email: itservicedesk@organisation.com (for reporting of non-urgent incidents only)

3.2 Major incident management and invocation of the IT service continuity plan

In the event of an incident that causes significant business disruption, the major incident process is initiated. Communication to impacted users will be from the IT service desk, either by means of email or telephone, to key business users at all affected sites. Regular updates will be provided hourly or more frequently, depending on the nature and status of the incident.

All priority 1 incidents as agreed against the SLA will be managed by a dedicated incident manager throughout the life cycle of the incident. The incident manager will follow the major incident management process, ensuring that:

- swift communication and effective updates are supplied to the business;

- the incident is managed effectively;
- a timely resolution is found.

Once resolved, the major incident manager will also provide a reason-for-outage report to the business within five working days, summarising the incident and actions to be taken as preventative measures in the future.

In the event that a major incident to the service necessitates a level of recovery that requires utilising the continuity environment, IT management, in conjunction with the business continuity management team, will invoke the IT service continuity plan.

The plan provides a method for invoking a failover of the production environment to the continuity environment and a basis for running services in this environment, perhaps at a reduced service level for an agreed period of time.

3.3 IT services response and target fix times

Table 3.1 shows the response and target fix times for Gold, Silver and Bronze services by priority.

Table 3.1 Incident response and target fix times

Service level standard	Gold		Silver		Bronze	
Incident priority	Response	Fix	Response	Fix	Response	Fix
P1	15 minutes	4 hours	15 minutes	6 hours	30 minutes	8 hours
P2	30 minutes	6 hours	30 minutes	8 hours	30 minutes	3 days
P3	2 hours	3 days	4 hours	5 days	4 hours	10 days
P4	4 hours	5 days	1 day	10 days	1 day	10 days

Note: Response = IT resolver group (for example, server support team) response to an incident in the form of a communication to the end-user acknowledging the incident and information on what steps are to be taken to resolve the incident, if they are known at that time.

3.4 Priority definitions

A priority value (1 to 4; see Table 3.2) is given to every incident to indicate its relative importance in terms of business impact and urgency, in order to ensure the appropriate allocation of resources and to determine the time frame within which action is required.

Table 3.2 Incident priority definitions

Priority	Business impact
Critical (P1)	Critical visibility incident such as any of the following: • nn users affected; • major impact on financial processes; • cost impact >£10,000; • services not available – no usable or productive workaround available.
High (P2)	Major visibility incident such as any of the following: • 25 to 49 users affected; • degradation in system response times or loss of system functionality; • moderate impact on financial processes, cost impact £2,000–10,000; • services partially unavailable for short periods.
Medium (P3)	Minor visibility incident such as any of the following: • 10 to 25 users; • minimum loss of system functionality; • minor impact on financial processes; • cost impact <£2,000.

(Continued)

Table 3.2 (Continued)

Priority	Business impact
Low (P4)	Limited or no visibility incident, where: • no direct impact on users or clients; • system resource low, but no impact yet; • reduced system capacity (e.g. emergency maintenance); • no impact on financial processes.

4. BUSINESS RESPONSIBILITIES

Business responsibilities and/or requirements in support of this agreement include the following.

- To facilitate restoration of IT service with minimal business impact within agreed SLA and business priorities, IT incidents should only be reported to the IT service desk.

- Availability of business process owners when resolving a service-related incident or request.

- The business requirements for new and modified IT services are subject to acceptance by IT governance and business sponsors. SLAs will be discussed and agreed at the start of the project.

- Attendance at monthly IT reviews with the SLM. Core business attendees are required to attend or assign a delegate to attend in their absence.

- Any increases to the current business unit personnel headcount (see Section 4.1 below) of 5 per cent or more must be communicated to IT service delivery in advance so that the potential impact on the agreed service levels in this document can be assessed.

- Participating in business continuity tests, as follows.

  - Availability of business process owners and/or service owners to participate in the tests.

  - Coordinate the business resources.

  - Execute the test as per the agreed test plan.

  - Produce the business report for business continuity management.

  - Planned test schedules will be agreed with the business one month in advance ensuring all third party obligations are incorporated and understood.

  - Production service failover to disaster recovery will be tested twice yearly.

- Supporting the IT security policy, as follows.

  - Interruptions to availability of a service due to non-compliance with the 'IT Acceptable Use Policy' are not covered by this agreement.

  - Compliance with the corporate security policy. Please refer to the following documents that are available on the corporate intranet:

    - IT Security Manual – all users

    - IT Acceptable Use Policy

    - IT Data Classification Policy

    - Fraud Policy and procedures

- Standards and guidelines on data protection are available on the corporate intranet from time to time and all signatories must undertake to review these documents, in particular data security breach management.

4.1 Sites/business functions covered by this agreement

Table 4.1 lists the sites/offices covered by this agreement.

Table 4.1 Sites within scope

Site (business function)	Site code	No. of Personnel
Head office	XXX	Nnn
Location 1	XXX	Nnn
Location 2	XXX	Nnn
Location 3	XXX	Nnn
Location 4	XXX	Nnn

5. KEY BUSINESS SERVICES

KBS 1
KBS 1 is the service that...

KBS 2
KBS 2 is the service that...

KBS 3
KBS 3 is the service that...

KBS 4
KBS 4 is the service that...

5.1 Service level standards

For further information, please refer to Table 2.1.

**Table 5.1 Key business services'
service level standards**

Services	Service level standard
KBS 1	Gold
KBS 2	Gold
KBS 3	Gold
KBS 4	Silver

5.2 Key services reporting

Service reports will be made available on a monthly basis and will be issued prior to the monthly service review chaired by the SLM. The reports will detail performance against service levels in addition to key metrics, such as those contained in Table 5.2, that the business depends on to perform vital business functions.

Table 5.2 Key performance measures

Business service	Key performance measures
KBS 1	Measure 1 Measure 2
KBS 2	Measure 1 Measure 2
KBS 3	Measure 1 Measure 2
KBS 4	Measure 1 Measure 2

The adoption of new metrics will be based on criteria such as whether they are required by the business, whether they are measured each month and whether the necessary toolsets/ skills are in place to capture such metrics.

APPENDIX B: SERVICE LEVEL MANAGEMENT PROCESS POLICY

It is a core tenet of ITIL that to be under control, a service management process requires three things:

- a process owner accountable for the process;
- a process policy that describes the organisation's framework for managing the process;
- a set of clear objectives for the process.

At a high level, ITIL describes what needs to be done to keep processes and activities under control. Being a generic framework intended to be applicable to all organisations in all industry sectors of all sizes and operating in both commercial and non-profit making environments, ITIL is less specific on how these activities should be managed. The reason for this is that organisations can adopt the generic framework but should tailor it to their specific needs.

The policy document that is a basic prerequisite for each process therefore describes how the process will operate specifically for your organisation. It is created and owned by the process owner. The intention of this section is to provide guidance on the contents and structure of the policy.

The purpose of the policy is to promote the efficient, effective and consistent application of good process practice throughout the organisation and wherever the process is undertaken. The management of the day-to-day process activities is the responsibility of the process manager or managers who will operate the activities in accordance with the policy.

An example policy document is shown below.

SERVICE LEVEL MANAGEMENT PROCESS POLICY

Purpose

The purpose of this policy is to promote the efficient, effective and consistent application of leading practice principles to the organisation's service level management activities as contained within the ITIL framework.

This policy therefore describes how the organisation's service level management activities will be conducted wherever they occur. This will ensure a standard approach that represents the optional methods that the organisation deems appropriate for its needs.

Scope of service level management

The scope of the service level management process includes the following activities:

- defining and documenting customers' service level requirements;
- analysing and reviewing the requirements to derive the feasibility, cost and time frame to meet the requirements and to determine the dependency on other internal functions and external organisations;
- negotiating the service levels applicable to each service;
- constructing the service level agreements (SLAs) and operational level agreements (OLAs) with internal departments, and contracts with external supplier organisations;
- provisioning support to supplier management to ensure that supplier contracts are aligned with the service levels in the SLA;
- assisting with the design and maintenance of the service catalogue;

- monitoring, measuring and reporting of service level achievements;

- conducting service review meetings with business representatives to identify improvement opportunities for inclusion on the CSI register and managing appropriate service improvement programmes;

- developing and documenting contacts and relationships with the business, customers and other stakeholders, in cooperation with business relationship management;

- logging and managing complaints and compliments, in coordination with business relationship management;

- updating or renegotiating the SLAs at the request of either party or in response to an external trigger;

- periodically reviewing the SLAs for relevance and applicability and revising the SLAs as necessary;

- terminating an SLA.

Objectives of service level management

The objectives of the process are as follows.

- Define, document, agree, monitor, measure, report and review the level of IT services.

- Provide and improve the relationship and communication with the business and customers in conjunction with business relationship management.

- Ensure that specific and measureable service levels are developed for all IT services (as defined in the service catalogue).

- Monitor and improve customer satisfaction with the quality of service delivered.

- Ensure that IT and the customer have a clear and unambiguous expectation of the level of service to be delivered.

- Ensure that even when all agreed service levels are met, the levels of service delivered are subject to proactive, cost-effective, continual improvement.

SLA structure

SLAs will be customer-based, that is, there will be one SLA per customer, to include all of the services used by that customer. In addition, each customer SLA will include information about the corporate services available to all customers.

Process activities

The activities associated with the process are shown in Figure 1. It also defines the responsibilities of the various stakeholders.

[Figure 1 would be a process flow chart included here, with swim lanes to indicate responsibilities.]

Key performance indicators

The key performance indicators (KPIs) that are used to measure the performance of the process are as follows:

- percentage of business units with whom IT has a signed and current SLA;
- percentage of services in the service catalogue for which there is an SLA;
- percentage of service review meetings conducted on time in the last 12 months;
- percentage of SLAs that have been reviewed at least once in the past 12 months;
- percentage of SLA reports issued on time in the last 12 months;
- number of customer complaints received in the last 12 months concerning the service level management process;

- percentage reduction in service levels missed over the last 12 months;

- percentage reduction in service levels missed over the last 12 months that were attributable to third party suppliers;

- percentage increase in the survey responses that indicate satisfaction, or better, with the process.

Roles and responsibilities

[The relevant roles and responsibilities would be defined here, including SLM, customers, supplier manager and so on.]

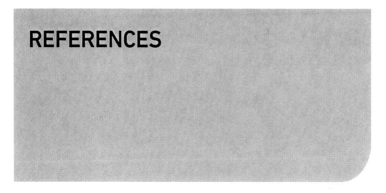

REFERENCES

Brewster, Ernest (2014) *Business Relationship Manager: Careers in IT service management* (BCS Guides to IT Roles). Swindon: BCS, The Chartered Institute for IT.

International Organization for Standardization (2012) ISO/IEC 20000-2:2012: Information technology – Service management – Part 2: Guidance on the application of service management systems. Geneva: International Organization for Standardization.

SFIA (2015) Skills Framework for the Information Age (SFIA) V6. London: SFIA Foundation.

Whapples, David (2015) *Continual Service Improvement Manager: Careers in IT service management* (BCS Guides to IT Roles). Swindon: BCS, The Chartered Institute for IT.

INDEX

Page numbers in *italics* refer to figures and tables

CPSIA information can be obtained
at www.ICGtesting.com
Printed in the USA
LVOW10s153827031B

571329LV00013B/571/P